Selfish'ism

Selfish'ism

Get up off your deathbed and save yourself
brother. I had to and so do you.

First Edition
(N^{th} I-nstallment)

Gary Dean Deering
(aka the world's first PsycHHology Engineer)

RaIse Books, LLC / Publisher / St. Paul

First edition, February 2013

Created in the United States of America
RaIse Books, LLC / Publisher
St. Paul, MN 55126

Cover Design by Gary Deering

Library of Congress Control Number: 2013901787

ISBN 978-0-977-49961-8

To Ayn Rand who *saved* my mind.

And others (next page).

To Dr. Leonard Peikoff and his writings and especially his *Analytic-Synthetic Dichotomy* article that single handedly *uncrooked* well over half of my 17 years worth of American-Public-Education-induced, intellectually *twisted*, psycho-epistemology.

To Dr. Nathaniel Branden and his Books *and* Intensives that *saved **me***.

And finally, **To** (the thirtysomethings) **Me** who *restarted* his development towards ***volitional*** *self-regulation* with this (his) *virginal* LTE (Letter-To-the-Editor) from a February past:

Dear Editor *The Minneapolis Star*:

I read with interest the article <u>Struggle expected before U.S. gets National Health Insurance</u> in the February 7 edition of your paper.

I am reminded how easy, how struggle-less, life would be if it were not for those selfish few, whoever they are, who insist on fighting for their rights at the expense of society's right to be taken care of by the federal government.

I just do not understand why some people think individuals have rights that supersede those of society. Where in god's name did they ever get such a notion. I thought everyone accepted, as universal truth, that like the sun, by its nature, is the base and source of energy on earth, so society, by its nature, is the base and source of mans rights on earth.

I will go so far as to grant to that troublemaking, selfish minority that this country was founded on

the *love* for individual rights. But then, he has to grant me the fact that for some time now it has been run on the principle of majority edict (if 6 out of 10 people determine by vote that the earth is flat, it is flat damn it --the other four are just deluded). I suspect those same four guys are responsible for the struggle referred to in the article.

Nonetheless, we are still a democratic nation. So, I think President Carter should change his words concerning the insurance coverage from *'universal and mandatory'* to *individual and voluntary*. Then the government should divide the projected cost of 100 Billion plus dollars by the 200 million plus people who will be covered by it and send them their bill in the mail requesting their *voluntary* contribution.

I then can send my $2000, four member family bill back, stamped --

Kiss My Ass!

Sincerely yours,

Gary D. Deering
2/ 7/ 77

(unpublished-LTEs/President Carters National Health)

{"published" here—<(unpublished LTEs)>/<(President Carter's National Health)>—some twenty years later: http://www.gdeering.com/GarysVenns/text/default.htm }

Prologue

The most common response—both Secular and Religious—to this book's call to action is:

Save yourself from what?

The Religionist's answer is:

From the Devil.

The Secularist's answer is:

From Religion.

If you have succumbed to Religion's Creed of Self-Sacrifice then you have succumbed to the devil and you have some issues to work out.

Not the least of which is the issue of Self Responsibility.

At the end of the day we are each responsible for our self; no one can take this fact away from us.

Nor should we want them to.

To selfish man, the fact of self responsibility is reason to rejoice.

To make the connection that by nature we are self responsible is gloriously good news because one thing we know for absolute sure about (mother) nature is that she doesn't do anything half way. If nature demands self responsibility of us then nature gives us all the tools we need to achieve a state of full and complete self responsibility.

Our job is to achieve it.

This book will help you do your job.

Gary Deering, Author

Contents

INTRODUCTION TO NOMENCLATURE

Selfishness as a virtue is alive.

Psychology as a science is dead.

Selfish'ism as a self help book is critical reading in the battle to keep your mind for yourself and not give it away willy-nilly to those others who want it in order to control you.

Selfish'ism, qua primer on *true* Scientific Psychology, is the foundation for our future investigations into three areas of its sphere of influence in our lives: *Psychhology Engineering, Theoretical Psych(h)ology and Teleömetrics (the mathematics of introspection)*.

Since Psychology as a science is dead some say it was never born.

So they—those same some—ask: so how could it be dead?

Answer: by virtue of the fact that it refuses to study the proper phenomenon in reality.

As long as psychology—that is, one 'h' psychology—insists on studying the wrong things, it will always lead to a dead end.

Always.

Human Beings with human consciousness are the right things to study.

Of course, for the broadest science, all living things that possess consciousness (awareness) are the right things to study.

For this reason I am designating real psychology, scientific psychology to be two 'hh' psychhology with the capitalized version—i.e., PsycHHology—to be a specialty inside the broader two 'hh' psychhology field.

That is, PsycHHology is all about Human PsycHology.

I use two 'hh' psychhology and one capital 'H' PsycHology interchangeably and by these I mean the science as started and defined by the Father of Modern (non-contemporary, non-dead) Psychology—Dr. Nathaniel Branden. In his seminal work on Theoretical Psychology—*The Psychology of Self Esteem*—first published by Nash Publishing in 1969, Dr. Branden defined psychology as: ... *the science that studies the attributes and characteristics that certain living organisms possess by virtue of being conscious.*

This definition is tomorrow's psychology today.

Today's psychhology is our now salvation.

Nomenclature

A in the formula A = A stands for each and every existent in each and every universe (if it turns out there are multiple universes inside the one and only Existence).

color as writing/communication tool … e.g., words of one color as means to emphasizing the word and also multi-colored words, e.g., *personal* as an attempt to visualize "integration" in addition to emphasizing the particular word. For example, the "integrated person" is *one* something but he or she is something made up of more than *one* thing even if we can't (yet) articulate what all those things are—vis-à-vis the literal rainbow revealing all the beautiful, actual *subparts* of sunlight.

DIM Hypothesis – **D** isintegration, **I** ntegration, **M** isintegration; Ayn Rand's intellectual heir Dr. Peikoff's nutshelled view of intellectually *developing* man and the hazards he faces. See Glossary.

Dreams … beyond our current scope but from a psych(h)ology point of view—or more precisely, psych(h)otherapy point of view—dreams can be very useful so we need to … use them. For now see **Glossary** under *consciousness* and consider it as a *node* for the f.u.t.u.r.e. of dreams.

FOF – *Facts on File*, a collection of information demonstrating to my readers that I'm not making the *particular* FOF_n tagged stuff up; ref. Appendix A.

f.u.t.u.r.e is mine—my *specific* future ***as will be determined*** by me **now** and my **now** choices—including my course correction choices now and in the future. (Inside the physical context of course of me living at an outpost solar system inside the galaxy named after a candy bar, on the 3rd rock from said solar system's sun along with other humans also so living and their f.u.t.u.r.e.s). See **w.o.r.d.s** below.

hgtikoi – pronounced "high-coy" with the intention of making your *mind* – after the fashion of a tuning fork – *resonate* to the concept of *haiku* which by association to its Eastern guru-like observations and pronouncements conjures up the quickie thought: '*profundity is about to follow*'. (And notice the assumed—on my part—*value* we share: both of us—me as author you as reader—believe that *profundity—an observation of reality that is true and insightful*—is possible and good. And even if for you, qua reader, it might not be achieved in the next "high-coy" opportunity **to** experience it we still *value* it and will look for it elsewhere and may even try and create it ourselves … for ourselves if for no other reason.)

I use 'high-coy' as a kind of sidebar—one that uses pink and gray and braces as the "bars":

hgtikoi{{{… content in gray … }}}

h-g-t-i-k-o-i stands for "*hey guys this is kind of important*" and it is from a client of mine whose name shall remain anonomous where she relayed a story about her two year old that was quite a precious story about two year olds – kids not only say the darndest things they also reveal so much. It was uttered to her and others driving in their car, she said, by her two year and 7 months old daughter. (See Glossary for story/context.)

ISBN – *International Standard Book Number*, a unique numeric commercial book identifier of either 10 or 13 digits. Their controlled issuance is country specific. In the United States the issuance is done and controlled by the private company, R. R. Bowker. ISBN's cost money to procure and use for published works.

jfk ... not capitalized JFK which usually stands for John Fitzgerald Kennedy, the 35th president of the United States of America, but rather lower case jfk as in: jesus-f'g-ka'rist! ... an *inner* incredible incredulity of mine that can be serious or tongue-in-cheek that pops to the forefront of me when I become aware of some really weird/bazar mental connection I'm making or trying to make or also when I become aware of some bad thing and/or stupid thing or rather some *incredibly* bad and/or *incredibly* stupid unbelievable thing that some person (including me, myself sometimes) did do ... or felt ... or advocates doing or thinking. *For example* the following was inside my head only, until here; as in, in order to show you what I mean I have to write it out into existence where you can see it:

'**jfk** you don't think that in the movie *Seven* (New Line Cinema film, written by A. K. Walker, released 1995) where *evil* triumphs over *good* that *I* am going to think it a good movie!?!?!?!? Do you actually think that I am going to agree with all those c*!ks#!&s who say it is a good movie?!?!?!?!?!? Well ... no f'g way hoe-zay. *Seven* is now number 15 on my list of 10 worst films of all time. The movie is evil and no amount of Ayn Rand compassion—i.e., I greatly disliked it but on it's own terms ... etc. ...—is going to change me because such compassion in this context is pure bullshit. *Seven* is such an evil f'g movie I can't seem to get it out of my craw by saying so a million times. Seven is evil ... seven is evil ... seven is evil ... seven is evil ... s top.'

I'm sure you get my drift.

(**PS:** Also notice the timelessness of inner mental contents ... Time doesn't heal all things, **I** heal all things. Except in this one *particular* case I had a little help from one of my older sisters. At the time of the movie I was only 50 years old and when I talked to her on the phone in general chit chat and I mentioned that contrary to public sentiment I for one did not like the movie, my sister—with a *tone* of bigger sister taking care of her little brother—said;

"Nobody liked that film." To which she to this day has no clue as to how high she rocketed in my hierarchy of valuable-to-me people when she said this. At the time I needed to hear it. And apparently as it now—January 2, 2013—turns out she wasn't the only clueless one because as I wrote this and everytime I reread it at the phrase 'bigger sister taking care of her little brother' I break into tears. Wow!!! I must say, the *commitment* to unobstructed awareness sure is … interesting.)

kjv – shorthand for g**KJV** which is *my* interpretation of the King James Version of *The Holy Bible* which is *one* version of the Christian's Holy Bible.

PS, PPS, PPPS … etc. … FPS: My favorite writing *form* is the personal letter. Consequently, this is a form I use a lot and part of the letter form is the concept of PS for Post Script as afterthought to the main body of writing. I have taken this to its ultimate: PS, PPS, PPPS etc. but not PPPPPPPPP….PPPPPP etc. S but usually end it long before this many P's with this concept: **FPS** as in, Final Post Script. So that, by PS, I mean usual Post Script and PPS I mean second Post Script and/or if applicable Post Script to the previous Post Script (as determined by context) and so on down to the ultimate, final postscript, FPS, as means to *ending* a particular writing harvest of the bountiful bounty in my mind (bountiful of course as I see it).

psychology – contemporary psychology; by *contemporary* psychology I mean the psychology view that is **supported *and* funded** by a country's government. See BiO Spiritualism's March 27, 2012 Newsletter (doorsign.biz) and Glossary herein for more information.

psycHology – the ***Biocentric Psychology*** of Dr. Nathaniel Branden, author of *The Psychology of Self Esteem* et al. whom—I predict—historians in the future will label: the

Galileo *and* Newton all rolled into one Scientist-father-founder of the **true** *Science of Psychology.*

hgtikoi{{{If I try to put these two together: Galileo + Newton and get *Galiton* and then stand back and look at it and it looks like, Galt … does that mean this is how Ayn Rand came up with the name John Galt in her magnum opus *Atlas Shrugged*? "John" is as about an American a name as you can get and Galt stands for Galileo & Newton all rolled into one? Or is this just an example of what is known as, a coincidence? And if it isn't a coincidence is it an example of psycho-hermeneutics—qua inner sub process of the art function—in action? See **Yes** in Glossary and specifically Chapter 17 therein for more.}}}

psycHHology – Human part of the phenomenon of psycHology taken by itself independent of any sub-human-animal subparts (e.g. Humans, qua humans, have a *sense* of humor but animals below us do not.)

Selfish'ism … is the *name* of the PROCESS of saving yourself from the Altruism philosophy. (See Glossary, Altruism.)

SVTOUL – Spiral Vortex Theory of UnLearning. See Glossary.

TLC – Tender Loving Care (see Glossary for more).

w.o.r.d.s – letters of special words separated by periods to indicate the suggestion of a subtext meaning—i.e. read between the letters—and/or of explanation of the concept by the meaning given by the individual using it to the word's individual letters, e.g., see T.H.E.Y in Chapter 1. Also this *dot notation* is used to highlight a particular concept in its word form that flags it a *potential* candidate to be figured out in the f.u.t.u.r.e. For example see **s.k.y** in Chapter 11 which when first invoked I did not know what it meant and then by the time I got around to writing the glossary I did. (First, see the first page of Chapter 11 then go to its point in the Glossary).

yu – see Glossary

Preface

Some might say that by using "Selfish'ism" rather than *Selfishness* I am succumbing to the Professional Objectivist's scaredy-cat ways where *they* use *neither* selfishness nor selfish'ism but rather *egoism* as the thing about which *their Philosophy of Objectivism* is all about.

Those who (might) say this might be right but ...

But what? Right is right and wrong is wrong so why the but?

Because, given the massive failure of my original sole proprietorship—The *Selfishness Training Institute* that could only garner 6 responses out of 1050 snail-mail solicited people with each and every one of those responses a negative (selfishness hating) response—to tout *selfishness* as the thing, the deal, the big kahuna is *impractical*. (Though I wonder now, if I mailed out that same solicitation today—that is, approximately a quarter of a century later—would the results be the same? Based on those cultural winds blowing through the sieves in my cognitive-neuroscience-psychology brain-head I'm speculating here that the *selfishness* tout is *still* impractical.)

And since the moral and the practical are the same thing, so too the *immoral* and the *impractical*. Voila! My selfishness *touting* is (was?) immoral.

Well, maybe that is a bit strong, so let's just say, maybe the *Selfish'ism* tout, for now, is *better* than the *selfishness* tout and that letting ones cognitive-neuroscience-brain-head *inform* one of anything is what is wrong.

So since I just discovered this new concept *Selfish'ism* (circa December 2011) and I am already (now, January

2012) beginning to think it is a really (really) good concept I am beginning to really really like the *word*.

Selfish'ism is you and me and any and each individual APPLYING the philosophy of "egoism" to our own self.

*Selfish'ism is **applied** egoism.*

Selfishness is *successful* selfish'ism.

When selfish'ism *succeeds* in *applying* egoism to the self in such a way so as to optimize self's happiness, selfishness is the result.

That is, *Selfishness* is *always* the *ideal* model to be built.

We are not trying to build a better horse drawn carriage here but we are still trying to build the first car – the model T if you like.

Just as some (literal) cars are better than others – e.g. The Porsche® (any model) is better than The Model T – so too are individual successes at building the ideal selfish soul rankable—both within and without: within *the* self and across the *individual* diversity of selves.

If one needs a euphemism for selfishness—that is, for the **one** that is in the assertion: **Selfishness** *is a virtue*—then one should use one that can be seen as a step in the *process* of becoming ever more selfish (that is, ever more moral, that is, ever more happy).

Hence *egoism* and *selfish'ism* are ok euphemisms to use for now but SELFISHNESS, qua virtue—we must never ever never never forget—is the goal.

Selfishness **is** a virtue.

—Author Gary (Dean) Deering,
the world's first formal PsycHHology Engineer

PART 1:

At the deathbed of your mind

"I am speaking at the deathbed of your mind, at the brink
of that darkness in which you are drowning, ...
The word that has destroyed you is,
'sacrifice'."

—Galt's Speech,
from *Atlas Shrugged* by
Ayn Rand, 1957, Random House,
New York, 18th Printing, hardcover, p. 1027

Chapter 1

T.H.E.Y

In a world that seems forever determined to deliberately destroy the individual's ego (if you doubt this, watch and listen to any of the Sunday morning clergy preaching to their faith-filled-flocks on TV once a week every Sunday Morning, week-in and week-out, week-after-week-after-week, 52 times a year, year-in and year-out, year-after-year-after-year; and/or look at Muslims who do the same kind of thing to themselves five times a day, day-in and day-out, day-after-day-after-day, Monday through Sunday for a minimum total of 35 times a week 1,820 times a year, year-in and year-out, year-after-year-after-rocking-back-and-forth-and-back-and-forth-in-the-never-ending-cycle-of-deliberately-destroying-egos-year) you have to preserve yours—or if necessary, resurrect yours—which is to say:

> In a world (of the man-made) that is forever determined to deliberately destroy egos you preserve yours by starting and/or continuing to build your ego strength through ego-exercises (in the choice to exercise my capacity to think or not to exercise it, I choose to exercise it), then move on to increase your selfishness strength through selfishness-exercises (in the choice to feel or not to feel I choose to actually feel what *my* capacity to feel is feeling) and then go back-and-forth and back-and-forth in your own rational TFA (ThinkingFeelingActing) defensive countermeasures for self preservation, spiraling higher and higher

      beyond your destroyers reach and into the
      lap of your own luxurious being.

People who accept as the truth, the whole truth and nothing but the truth the claim that self-sacrifice is the highest ideal, end up being dedicated to destroying egos, to killing egos because ego is the only thing standing between them and their vision of a perfect world. By their own past choices they have no current choice not to destroy egos (their future choices of course are still open, albeit, in inverse proportion to the degree of their "success"—high success at destroying their own ego, low desire to not destroy yours). Granted they all start with their own ego first and some never fully succeed in destroying it, but others of t.h.e.m do and so upon t.h.e.i.r success at destroying their own ego, t.h.e.y then are compelled to destroy yours least you remind them of the actual evil they have committed (against themselves) and so it becomes t.h.e.i.r mission in life to destroy you.

You as that inner three-dimensional-psycHological-mirror that T.H.E.Y can't stand to stand in front of. To do so is to face you: yu the judge, yu the jury and yu the executioner.

This is not fiction.

This is observable fact.

Introspectively observable fact.

For this reason t.h.e.y are actively against introspection.

To preserve and protect your own ego becomes your immediate job and so in this regard you have to become your own policeman; an internal policeman dedicated to protect and serve: to protect your ego and serve your self.

Make no mistake about it, t.h.e.y are out to get you.

But.

Make not another mistake either. T.h.e.y are so easy to defeat it is almost a joke to even view them as an adversary once you see through t.h.e.i.r ways.

Granted, T(hey)H(ave)E(vil)Y(earnings) but since *true* evil is the absence of *true* good, to make the *real* good present in you all you have to do is *worship* reason and freedom.

Once this is done, T.H.E.Y are done.

Chapter 2

I virtue

Selfishness worships reason and freedom.

Selfishness is a virtue and like all virtues it is not an easy thing to acquire.

It seems as if vices are easy, virtues hard.

In this context we could say, virtues are acquired, vices absorbed.

Absorbed from what? is a logical question to ask, as is, acquired how?

Since we are concerned with virtues, specifically the virtue of selfishness we will only spend a little bit of time answering the absorbed from what? question.

Vices are absorbed from the culture at large and they are a by-product of inadequate thinking and/or of not thinking and/or of irrational thinking.

Vices are a consequence of choosing not to exercise our capacity to think to its fullest extent within our growing context (see Chapter 6 for more).

Vices are a by-product of an open mind—a mind that is open but not active. Vices are the product of a mind open to any and all content but closed to any and all action of a certain kind in regard to the content—specifically, closed to the action-of-mind we call, *judging.*

This is why one of selfish man's conclusions is: the mantra, *judge not least ye be judged* ... is the mantra of an uncourageous mind, therefore, *judge and be prepared to be judged* is the mantra of a courageous mind.

Courage is better than cowardice, hence, being courageous is better than being cowardly. Courage is the ability to act on what you know is right even though all your significant others (all your "they") are telling you, you are wrong. (*Not* acting on what you know is right is dangerous; acting on what you know is wrong is deadly for your ego.)

The inadequate thinking or non-thinking absorbed vices can be easier to undo than the irrational thinking "absorbed" ones because the latter have more of an acquired—read, "rationalization"—taste to them than do the others.

Acquired implies choice and involves will, purposeful action, purposefully chosen action or what we call, volition.

Acquired tastes are more deeply ingrained and hence more difficult to change. In fact there often is no desire to change them because they are experienced as "just me", my identity, who I am, my essence and as such are what we could call, again in this context, "hard wired" by us into our psyche.

hgtikoi{pronounced high-coy{{But don't forget: soldered wires can be reheated and un-soldered also.}}}

Since selfishness means being concerned with meeting our own survival needs—including the long run need to thrive *and* prosper—we have to continue asking logical questions in order to understand and acquire the virtue of selfishness.

To this end we have already asked the most important question: How is the virtue of selfishness acquired? albeit, we have not yet answered it.

Before we can there are other questions to ask and answer.

What does the word virtue mean?

What does the word vice mean?

Virtue is the constellation of actions that we personally engage in to obtain our cardinal values.

Vice is the constellation of actions we engage in that prevent us from obtaining reality matching—that is, objective—cardinal values.

hgtikoi{{{When *our* "virtues" become vices—or vice reversa—is the exact instant when we *know* that in regards to the slippery slope, *we have slipped*.}}}

Cardinal values means most-important-to-our-life values.

We humans hold our cardinal values at the core, the center of our being.

We hold the rest of our values radially outward from this core with some kind of a personal importance-at-a-distance-from-the-core formula that only our *inner* know-it-all-(about us)-*god* knows.

Though it is knowable, we don't have to know this formula exactly in order to pursue our values.

As human beings with a human nature, pursuing values is what we do.

A value is something—anything and everything—we act to gain and/or keep. Values are the objects of action.

hgtikoi{{{**Action** here means both mental and physical, e.g., when we **value** self awareness and/or self acceptance and/or self assertion we spend **mental action obtaining** and/or **maintaining** and/or **increasing** our self awareness and/or self acceptance and/or self assertion **abilities**.}}}

Values as objects can change or stay the same and new ones can be sought after and old ones decommissioned.

We as human beings with a human nature have this kind of a relationship with values.

In this sense then, we are our values and our values are us.

Values are changeable, hence so are we.

That is, if we put our mind to it we can acquire the virtue called selfishness.

As human beings who must meet their needs in order to survive, we should be selfish.

As human beings who do have needs that have to be met and the capacities to meet them, we should consider it of the utmost in selfishness for us to know just exactly what those capacities are and how they work.

That is, we humans should have shoulds.

We just have to learn which shoulds we should have and which shoulds we shouldn't have—and once we do we will be selfish.

That is, virtuous.

So that when "they" say of us: "He (she) is selfish.", they will be paying us a tribute we have earned, not a compliment we don't deserve.

Chapter 3

Selfishness and The Science of Becoming

Selfishness means being concerned with ones own needs so much so that he or she will do all that it takes to meet them knowing that if they don't meet them they will die.

If we don't meet a "need" and we don't die—be it now or within a human time frame that could be classified as long, albeit, not lifelong—then it wasn't a need. When we add to this the concomitant idea of "not-meeting and not-being-debilitated as a consequence of not meeting" then we have an example of a needs test: *meet our needs, we live; don't meet them, we die.* We die either quickly or slowly with the degree of debilitating pain proportional to the speed of death—instantaneous death, no pain; slow and drawn out death, lots of pain. Or when we do meet our needs we live now and for sometime to come with the degree of motivating pleasure proportional to the speed of life—instantaneous life, i.e., that last sex was pret-ty g.dd... good, to the careful ingredient selection ... slow and drawn out preparation simmer ... of a top chef's TLC to cook up ... a happy life. So that, *absent* all-of-the-above in the presence of some "thing" others have told us is a "need", simply means that in at least this one instance, we have been misinformed.

Speaking of needs then we can add this hypothesis: pleasure and pain are needs but in a special way. Pleasure is a need, but it is not always needed. Pain on the other hand is always needed, but it is not a need.

That is, pleasure is a need, but it is not always needed immediately. Pain is not a need, but it is always needed when appropriate and when appropriate sooner is better than later.

Selfishness is big in the degree of its concern about pleasure and pain; self*less*ness is big in the degree of its unconcern about pleasure and pain.

Self*less*ness is such a big unconcernedness that those who are selfless aren't even concerned about their own pleasure needs so as to try and satisfy them.

Self*less*ness means not being concerned with ones own needs enough to even try and identify them let alone try and satisfy them.

Self*less*ness means having a *passive* relationship between ones own needs and ones own actions *required* to satisfy them.

Selfishness—on the other hand—means having a *passionate* relationship between ones own needs and ones own actions required to satisfy them.

Selfish people are passionate about the self and if they do it right they will end up being truly happy.

Selfless people are impassionate about the self and are incapable, by that very choice, to do the right thing and so they will never be happy. They will never be happy because by their own choice they cannot—all things staying constant—they *metaphysically cannot* be happy— happiness being a state of non-contradictory joy.

Joy and suffering are not the same thing. Joy comes from satisfied needs, suffering from unsatisfied needs.

Metaphysically, doing the right thing and doing the wrong thing do not produce the same consequences.

hgtikoi{{{ (YouCanTestThisYourSelf: Bake your next cake *not* in a medium temperature oven but in your oven

while it is in self-clean mode—compare result to your
other baked cakes.)}}}

Right and wrong are not the same thing.

Neither is good and evil.

Right and wrong are opposites; good and evil are polar
opposites.

The equator band between them is the *not good* and the
bad, as—respectively—*right* side, *wrong* side equator
straddlers. The "not-good" touches the equator band on
the polar-good side of the sphere and the "bad" touches the
equator band on the other, polar-evil side of the equator.
In this context 'right' is on the side of good and 'wrong' is
on the side of evil.

As it must be; as it should be—aspiring selfish man's
problem is to figure out the true meaning of 'right' and
'wrong' and 'good' and 'evil' so that he does not end up
with a deformed sphere.

If man's core were a static sphere, then the preceding
imagery would describe it three dimensionally. The two
dimensional description of cardinal core values surrounded
by many many many concentric circles of diminishing
value to-the-self's life values as they travel outward from
the core—like the ripples from a stone thrown into a pond
into the exact same spot as the last thrown stone just before
its ripples died out—would describe it dynamically.

In the static view, whether the good is your north pole and
the evil your south or the good is your south pole and the
evil your north is a completely idiosyncratic point and has
no practical, hence, no moral impact on our emerging
psycHological model.

Selfishman is born selfish, albeit, not selfishman.

He is rather—speculation has it—born a "one-with-the-universe" sensory-perceptual, directly-experiencing-existence baby-bundle with the power of awareness we call human consciousness. (This is theoretical extrapolation as to what our power of awareness must be like at the beginning of our development: we simply are aware of all the things out there we can be aware of that come within our purview—all the things that stimulate our senses—but we haven't yet figured out where the "out there" ends and where the "in here" begins because there is no out there or in here there's only the things we are aware of, so, to repeat, at the beginning there is no separate 'we' and no separate 'things' there's only awareness of *all* 'things'.)

A baby so born that is on (as anyone can extro-and-retro-spectively observe) a final-causation mission to become an ego-self within two years (see the terrible two's) and a self with-a-strong-ego on or before his or her 5th birthday (see yourself introspectively at ages 3,4 and 5 or so—for me it was 5 or 6, for you it could be less or it could be the 'or so').

(As I observe in myself introspectively as I recall my early development years and hence know that you could too if you wanted to since you as a human being have access to the same inner laboratory about the world of *self* and *ego* that I do).

So that developmentally—dynamically—we can say that today's "egocentric" *child* is the son or daughter of tomorrow's selfish man or woman.

Egocentric *adults* on the other hand are not adult selfishman. In fact, egocentric adults give selfishness a bad name.

Egocentric adults are egocentric children who failed to completely complete (in a kind of self'ist-interruptus way) the *separation* & *individuation* part of the psycHological work required to become adult—read, autonomous—selfishman.

As a result, by the time such arrested development children are in their twentysomethings (yesterday's baby boomer generation; today's follow on generations are more like thirtysomethings) where they should be navigating—if they haven't already circumnavigated their own inner globe from programmed-to-volitional self regulation—where they should be navigating the *closeness* and *integration* parts of successful (read, authentic) self esteem development as same is prerequisite to becoming and being *autonomous*—that is, psycHologically developed healthy—man.

Later (Chapter 7/FOF$_3$) we introduce how to employ these (iterative) developmental steps—*closeness, separation, individuation* and *integration*—to becoming autonomous man which when combined with the spiritual desire to live life on earth as happy man constitutes all the process steps needed to becoming adult selfish man and close the circle on us succeeding in completing our psycHological growth and development job to becoming mature adult man.

After successfully reaching the adult plane of human existence then, all subsequent "psycHological" growth and development is really Spiritual growth and development and if our psycHological development was two times more complicated than we thought, the spiritual part is quadruply so and suffice it to say beyond the scope of our current interest.

(Consequently, I leave "it"—the development of (BiO) Spiritualism into a full blown science—up to the f.u.t.u.r.e me should I live long enough to so develop. That is, should I live to be, say, at least a 150 as I earlier promised my (now fortysomethings then) 6 year old and 10 year old daughters back in the day, that is, back-in-the-day when I personally went from being immortal-to-mortal.)

(Given the potential for bionic organ replacement therapy as means to human longevity, the 150 year old me isn't totally wishful thinking. Granted it is a bit of a stretch for me personally, but not for those somewhere in the age spectrum who are alive today. And so maybe I'll live long enough to grow in my knowledge and be able to finish what I've started here in regards to transforming "spiritualism"—*the **process** of making oneself the sole prideful owner of worthy and efficacious consciousness; a consciousness that is worthy of happiness BECAUSE it is competent at producing it*— into a full blown science.)

Or not as the case may be.

But for now—since we are still focused on our psycHological development—suffice it to say:

PsycHological development is work!

All selfish people exert the effort to develop psycHologically and all selfless people do not.

Selfishness is being concerned with ones own needs and values and acting in concert with those concerns.

Including the concern to get-it-right.

Or we should say, *especially* the concern: to get it right.

We say "especially" out of deference to the irrefutable fact that man is not omniscient.

Selfish man first and foremost respects facts—any facts, all facts.

Fact: man is not omniscient.

Fact: man is not omnipotent.

Fact: man is not omnipresent.

Fact: man has volition.

Fact: man can learn.

Fact: man does learn.

Fact: man can know.

Fact: man does know.

Fact: gravity works.

Fact: the sun rises every day and sets every night.

Fact: man is responsible for himself.

That is, selfish man *accepts* the metaphysical fact of self responsibility whereas selfless man *rejects* it.

Notice, neither have a choice in being self responsible or not being self responsible; by nature each is self responsible as each is human and in human nature individual humans are responsible for the self. The choice is in accepting this fact or rejecting it.

To repeat, selfish man accepts it.

fa(IN)ct this is the basic meaning of the psycHological concept we call, *self-responsibility*—basic as in fundamental as in starting point: *I accept the metaphysical fact that I am responsible for myself.*

In similar fashion, self acceptance—that is, in the primal sense, *self acceptance*—is: *selfishness.*

And so in this primal sense *selfishness* is the opposite of *self rejection.*

Actually, *developmentally*, it is the other way around: self rejection is the di-polar—that is, *ultimate*, polar—*opposite* of self acceptance.

hgtikoi{{{ Hence, theoretically, we speculate that *self-rejection* could be the pin-point source of **all** psycHological problems that affect individual humans via their failure to master the development of their own personal psycHology—a development that is far from automatic and is fraught with many hazards. See Dr. Peikoff's *The DIM Hypothesis* in Nomenclature and Glossary for such "occupational hazards" for *intellectually* developing man. To correct—that is, cure—such *psycHology* induced problems is reasonably easy to do. But discussion of this is beyond our current scope so we will pick it up again later—in some to be determined f.u.t.u.r.e book. }}}

Self acceptance and self rejection are the only two possible choices open to us—self indifference is not a metaphysically sustainable outcome as it eventually turns into self rejection. This is analogous to a mechanical column that carries an accumulating weight (self is responsible for more and more as the literal self ages) that gets so heavy that it eventually buckles. The column can't be "indifferent" to such a load, either it is made big enough (by us, qua acceptors of metaphysical facts) to handle the load or it buckles. A collapsed or collapsing psycHology—most commonly experienced as a crisis of self-esteem which can manifest itself as a collapsing or collapsed house-of-cards psychoepistemological-worldview that *is* irrational—is a possible—albeit, not inevitable, but possible—outcome for developing humans.

(Psychoepistemological structures can be rational or irrational, or more rational than irrational or vice versa depending on individual choices to make one's mental scaffolding—that is, one's psychoepistemology—be safe and secure rather than rickety and dangerous to climb as same is required from time-to-time to maintain and/or

repair one's epistemology. Though one's epistemology—
that is, psychoepistemology—is more difficult to change
than say, one's metaphysic it is nonetheless changeable
and if a person needs to improve his or her
psychoepistemology they just have to study formal logic
and introspection—intently. Study Formal logic to
discover all the errors in thinking that all human beings are
susceptible to—then *correct the ones that apply to you*;
study introspection to discover your own personal ego self
so that you know "who" to *apply* gained knowledge *to*.
Depending then on which psychoepistemological
structure—in balance—*you have made yours be*—house of
cards, house of straw or house of bricks—will "tell you" to
what degree you need professional help in preventing the
bromidic cultural winds from huffing and puffing and
blowing your house down and leaving you exposed to the
harsh realities that come from refusing to accept self
responsibility as a metaphysical fact. And, on the flip side,
once said fact is accepted, *your* achieving *your*
happiness—granting that once happiness is achieved your
continued growth in being human is completely up to you
and your choice to do it completely on your own or get
help or any combos thereof that you desire—is but a
heartbeat away.)

(For more on psychoepistemology see Chapter 9.)

Selfish man—by age 5—accepts the metaphysical fact of
self responsibility and along with it accepts the importance
of being self-accepting and accepts it so-much-so that he
makes self-acceptance be one of his cardinal values.

Self-less man on the other hand—if such is even possible
at this early an age—accepts none of it and begins
rebelling against his nature as selfishman rather than
embracing it.

(A rebellion based on volition or cultural osmosis or combos of both is really part and parcel of individual differences psycHology, so is beyond our current scope.)

For selfish man, acceptance does not mean condone, it means being one who accepts facts, facts being anything and everything that is true about reality.

Including the realities about one's self, e.g., don't jump out of this tree from this third big branch up here because it'll hurt; followed eventually with: if I jump off the top of this (Ranger) tower—here in Itasca State Park at the mouth of the Mississippi River where the 12 year old me along with other park visitors have climbed up into to see the forest below from the Ranger's perspective as I back away from the rail not sure about the degree of control I do or do not *yet* have over this inner ability TO CHOOSE my actions, e.g., if I choose to jump as a test—it'd probably kill me.

Bad test idea.

So since selfish man is now convinced that you can't have too much self-acceptance he concludes not only is the value of self-acceptance his cardinal value but that it is also an objective cardinal value.

A value is cardinal if it is held in our core and it is an objective cardinal value if it is an unconditional value and it is an unconditional value if in reality it is good for you and you can't have too much of it – e.g., health, *authentic* self esteem to name just two.

Self-acceptance to the selfish man is an objective, unconditional value and so selfish man in essence says, I *want* to be self-accepting.

And then does what is required to obtain the value of self-acceptance and ultimately automatizes the important actions required to so obtain and maintain this value and hence ultimately obtains the virtue of self-acceptance.

Selfish man then knows he achieves this state of self acceptance when he experiences beneficial differences in his personal life and well being from being this way.

And when in reality he does experience this, he takes the time to pause and acknowledge these benefits.

He reaches the ultimate in this achievement when he experiences the heat-of-pride warming his physical being to such a degree that he wants to conclude: life is easy—so what's all the fuss about?

But selfish man, being one who learns from his past experiences knows, since pride goeth before the rIse all he has to do is bask in the glow of his pride—as if it were a warm fire on a cold night—for as long as it lasts and then move on to other (pride producing) achievements.

That is, aspiring selfish man's work is not yet complete.

And we don't want to tell him just yet—least it be discouraging rather than animating as it will be by the time he discovers it for him/her self ... we don't want to tell them just yet that, selfish man's work is never done. Albeit, since reality always has the final say, selfishman's work is ultimately interrupted and ended.

We just want that "interruption" and end to occur some goodly amount of time after aspiring selfishman becomes self-esteeming selfishman.

Chapter 4

Self Esteem and The Art of Being

There are two types of self esteem: authentic self esteem and phony self esteem.

Selfish men and women want the authentic kind.

Aspiring selfish man knows when he himself is being phony and when he is being real—that is, authentic.

But since he is aspiring to the goal of selfishness and has not yet reached it he only knows this about himself to the same, exact degree he has made self-awareness a value.

Self-awareness is something human beings are capable of but other animals are not—that is, other animals do not have the capacity for self awareness but man does.

Self-awareness is a distinctly human attribute.

Self-awareness means that the person is aware of himself as a separate entity—a "thing"—in the world.

Self-awareness also means that the person is aware of his impact on the world—if he or she speaks loudly in a library others will shush him; if he or she whispers when asking for something they will usually hear, "speak up, we can't hear you!" as a reply. Or if he or she does some special feat of efficacy—wins lots of free games for himself on a real (or virtual) pinball machine, masters the art of riding a bicycle so that he can travel further and experience more in less time than it used to take walking—he will then feel a special kind of inner sensation that he will learn later in life is the feeling that adult human beings call pride. And he will also learn that the summation of a whole bunch of these efficacy driven feelings of pride is the source of his sense of "worth". Source that is, in the sense of *proof* that he, qua individual human being, has developed his human capacities to such a high degree that he can and does produce feelings of authentic pride in himself as a result of his accomplishments and as this same individual being, he is capable of basking in the glow of these accomplishments.

And of course, be able to use these accomplishments to satisfy future needs.

(For example, the future need to also be aware of the impact he or she has on him or herself when, for example, he or she thinks a certain thought and then asks: why did *my* mind *choose* this particular thought?)

Aspiring selfish man knows that efficacy and worth, pride and self esteem are all interrelated and that authentic self esteem awaits his knowing exactly how they are related.

This exactness has been given as a gift to aspiring selfish man—not by the gods, not by nature, but—by Dr. Nathaniel Branden, the Scientist's scientist on the subject of authentic Self Esteem when he, Dr. Branden said: "Self esteem is the reputation you acquire with yourself" and "Self esteem is saying, I can; pride is saying, I have." (For this and more, see all the works of Dr. Nathaniel Branden, especially: *The Psychology of Self-Esteem; Honoring the Self; The Six Pillars of Self-Esteem* and *The Disowned Self.*)

Selfishman is aware of his inner self enough to know when an abstraction has been properly concretized—that is, when it has been brought down to earth and made—by others and/or self—to have the certainty of sensory perceptions. That is, selfishman knows that in the foregoing, Dr. Branden's succinctness is right-on-the-money, i.e., is true.

Selfishman knows that "matches reality" and "is true" are simply two different ways of saying the same thing.

Consciousness or awareness of reality is something all living entities of a certain kind possess. That kind is the kind that moves through its environment satisfying its needs along the way.

Awareness is what consciousness *is*. *Identify* is what consciousness *does*.

Man's self-awareness is simply a subset of the broader capacity we call awareness.

Physical survival requires extrospective (out there) awareness to have metaphysical primacy over introspective (in here, self) awareness. And because of this and other to-be-identified-things, aspiring selfish man is-want to accept Modern Philosophy's (Objectivism's) claim that existence has *metaphysical primacy over consciousness*.

Aspiring selfish man notices that the counter claim—consciousness has metaphysical primacy over existence—is surely a possible thing to accept and since these two claims are exact opposites they can't both be true—either one is true and the other false, or both are false.

Aspiring selfish man accepts nothing on faith and wants only the truth—especially in fundamental issues such as the fundamental concerning man's proper relationship to reality, to existence.

We say "especially" out of deference to the irrefutable fact that some things are more important than other things—for example, at work the other day I forgot to dot an "i" in a hand note to a co-worker whereas a local Doctor/Surgeon I read about in my local newspaper operated on a patient and took out the wrong kidney. (The Doctor was reprimanded by his handlers—the State run medical community. I on the other hand, being an irrational objectivist, fired myself. However, later—after I discovered Biocentric psychology—I rehired me. This fabricated, made up example of my irrational moralizing against a non-i dotter—the story about the Doctor is true—is an example about a specific kind of psychoepistemological ~~corruption~~ error. Errors can become corruptions but they don't have to. They cross over the error/corruption line *at-the-exact same instant* when "they"—errors—become praised internally—by some "part" of us—as good or—just before the manner of a slippery slope near the equator of our polar sphere of good and evil—as ***not*** bad. That is, errors are bad, to label them "not bad" *is* slippery slope.)

hgtikoi{{{Is this meaning **that** of **rewriting** reality? – i.e.g., that one example Ayn Rand gave of herself when young and she became aware of her "jealousy" of prettier, glamorous girls her age and then in the next instance **rewrote** this to be: **not** jealousy but AR wanting to be glamorous. And if so, it—internally standing at the top of the slippery slope between error and corruption—**is** the *place* where **extremely** high intellectual honesty – such as that **developed** by AR **later** in life as she now represents the poster child for intellectual honesty — can save you from becoming corrupt ... that is? the reason?!?!?! you want to *make* intellectual honesty be a **cardinal value** is because you don't want to **become** corrupt ??? *Intellectual honesty* is the energy field *protecting* you from corruption's slings and arrows and ... in the 21st Century… from epistemological corruption's photon torpedoes being shot at you from every dummy down corner of the culture's too many corners to cut or count. That is, erring on the side of intellectual honesty is better for you than not? (For example, even though mmq'g—Monday Morning

Quarterbacking—works in football to help produce better football *players*, it does not work the same way in horse race betting—see my horse race mmq'g in the doorsign.biz archives from the times **before** I knew this—it does not work to produce better *horse-race-outcomePredictor-bettors*. Nonetheless, a *kind* of mmq'g here helps one maintain intellectual honesty and to this extent is good. That is, is good **if** you decide to try and get some **Recreational** benefit from betting on the horses then don't sell your soul to the devil of *only* remembering and/or touting the correct bets and forgetting the incorrect ones. Of course, don't do the reverse either.)}}}

<u>Yes</u>, some things are more important and aspiring selfish man knows that fundamentals—in relation to other things on nature's hierarchy—are such things.

Knowing this and other things then, aspiring selfish man starts the long, challenging, arduous journey to discover the truth about fundamentals in general and this: "existence has metaphysical primacy" fundamental, in particular.

In this situation he does the only thing adult human beings can do: he retreats to the cave in his mind and uses the all of his inductive and deductive powers to figure out what he thinks based on all his knowledge and logical thinking skills to be the truth about fundamentals.

That is, aspiring selfishman does the same in relation to his self-knowledge that he did for all his other knowledge—he grows in it at his own rate.

hgtikoi{{{a zero rate is not a rate and a negative rate is not growth}}}

Aspiring selfishman long ago accepted the premise that knowledge is possible, that man can know.

Since a big part of this retreating-to-the-cave metaphor *process* is sub-conscious and involves inner relationships between his conscious, volitional mind and his subconscious automatic mind, aspiring selfish man is not completely aware of the process (if he were completely or even significantly aware of this process he wouldn't be aspiring).

Depending upon his age at this particular retreat and the number of such retreats so far in his life, aspiring selfish man emerges some time later with the answers.

The answers—right or wrong, for better or for worse—are his and form the basis of what philosophy calls his metaphysics and his sense-of-life. (That is, his *answers* to the fundamental questions: Where am I? and Is it worth it? form the basis—e.g.: I'm on the third rock from the sun and you g.dd... right it is.)

Depending on the precision—or lack thereof—of his concepts and the degree of his *skill* in reasoning, aspiring selfishman's tomorrow mantra might be: back to the cave.

Or it could of course be: finally, I have arrived, I see what I see and I know what I know. Thank (the non-existent) god(s) for human consciousness in all its *glory*, that is, *integrated* parts—the conscious and the subconscious with all its individual human actualness and all its to-be-determined human potential.

But before selfishman can say the latter and especially the "I have arrived" he has to be able to say the "I".

That is, he has to be able to say, *I am me*.

Selfish man's development so far is only partially complete—he has achieved enough self-acceptance to advance his "me" concept but not yet enough self awareness so as to solidify it. And so far he hasn't even mentioned the concept of self-assertion let alone developed enough of it. Consequently, he can only think this "I am me" statement. If he says it out loud too soon it will have a ring of phoniness to it. (He might, for example, feel more "authentic" at this stage saying, I am on-track to becoming whom I—along with me, myself—*want* me to be.)

Since selfish man as we previously noted wants the real, the authentic and not the phony, not the unreal, he has to immerse himself more deeply into solving the problem of self-awareness or what is most commonly referred to as: the problem of introspection.

How do I become more introspective? aspiring selfishman asks himself.

By defining the term, comes the answer to selfishly developing self-aware man, so that I know or have some inkling where this particular journey is going to take me.

Introspection is a process of cognition directed inward.

That makes sense, extrospection is a process of cognition directed outward, so, voila! introspection is ... etc.

'Let this fun—albeit difficult—journey continue', says aspiring more-selfishness-man to so-far-developed-selfishman.

Chapter 5

The Art and Science of Being and Becoming

selfish is related to the second of (BiO) Spiritualism's Three P's (see Chapter 11).

Spiritualism's first P is P hilosophy's either/or discovery about good and evil. Since evil is the absence of the good, it is an either/or issue: either, you choose the good, or, you *get* the evil. (And for every *good* you do choose you lessen the potential for evil *to get* a potential.)

We of course choose the *good* (see Glossary).

And notice that in regards to Spiritualism's *second* **P** (**P**sychhology) it isn't so much an either/or choice as it is a both\and choice.

We have to master the art of being *and* becoming. It isn't being or becoming or becoming or being but it's both our being needs and our becoming needs that we have to meet. Meeting our being needs means achieving the goal of surviving and thriving for today and today only and enjoying the achieved goals in the here and now: eating todays meals, wearing todays clothes, living in todays house, driving today's car, enjoying today's sex, and other now needs. Meeting our becoming needs means growing and developing in our ability to survive and thrive for more than a day: enroll in college, sign up for a welding class, go to psychotherapy, join an exercise club, develop the ability to hold a rational perspective on our own *personal* future (f.u.t.u.r.e) and so on.

Sometimes being needs can overshadow becoming needs and vice versa. For example, right now in my own personal life as I am working on the manuscript for this book (7/22/2011) my becoming needs are overshadowing my being needs: I have an overriding need to get out from under my long term debt sooner rather than later as at my age I don't necessarily have a lot of four year plans left in me. This becoming is going to take about three more years (one miserable, one back to semi-normal, one—the last one—will be fun to euphoric): first year will be a balls-to-the-wall 100% reduction in *all* credit card debt, second year in other type debts and the third year will be devoted primarily to filling my own coffers so that I can completely enjoy a full time or near full time retirement for the next 39 years (or FTROML—ForTheRestOfMyLife—if same is greater than one year).

So when such an overshadowing event happens (independent of why it "happens" with the answer to the "why" question itself a becoming need to be satisfied *eventually*) we should take time away from the overshadowed needs and apply it to the problem of meeting the overshadowing needs with the goal of restoring the time balance between our becoming and being needs as soon as is humanly possible.

We *should* that is IF selfishness—being *concerned* with our own needs and values and *acting* in concert with those concerns—is our goal.

And it is.

hgtikoi{{{here is one area where selfishness shines in comparison to altruism as it, the selfishness ethic—once automatized into our personal code—is the only one of the two that has a prayer in hell of *successfully* applying the **Philosophical Principle** that states: ***the moral and the practical are the same thing***. This **principle** means that if some value or goal that we are **contemplating** achieving is

not moral than it is not practical and if it is not practical
then it is not moral—that is, it has to be *both* moral *and*
practical for it to serve our **authentically** selfish
interests.}}}

Selfishness we can argue requires two primary strengths:
courage and self assertion.

Epistemologically, courage is the easier of the two
strengths to deal with; to do so simply requires us to
remember the principle stated in Chapter 2: courage is
better than cowardice.

Courage is better than cowardice because cowardice means
we *never* act against fear and courage means sometimes—
when deemed appropriate by us to do so—we do act
against our fear.

Fear, like love, is an emotion.

As such, acting courageously is us implementing in
practice the moral (i.e. correct, i.e. true) premise that says,
emotions are not tools of cognition.

Applying this principle is part 'n parcel of the psycHology
of self (assertion) that we are trying to develop—
ultimately, we want a self that is courageous not cowardly.

As to self assertion, we can argue that there are two basic
types of self assertion: self assertion *insertion* and self
assertion *experiment.*

Self assertion *insertion*—you being you in the world—is
just that: you being you with each and every moment of
being. Of being a thinking, feeling, acting sentient being
in the world.

Self assertion *experiment* on the other hand is you
checking out your new ideas—as well as your old
premises—about what's what against the facts of reality by

controlling the time and the place and the nature of pre-
selected self-assertion-insertions. That is, by being from
time-to-time all-of-the-above sentient-being being *and* also
at-the-same-time being an observing, theorizing, testing,
judging sentient being in the world.

When you do both as described you are being *experimental*
(some call the experiences during this time, *experiential*)
and when you do it with eyes wide open you can learn a
great deal about yourself—your self qua human being with
a human nature, surviving and thriving in the world.

Insertion and experiment—developmentally—are leap frog
partners.

All of your self assertion insertions and experiments over
time constitute your developing self and at any given point
in time constitute your developed self up to and including
that point.

Your developed self is the locus of all such points.

At any given point in time you are actually—in the
details—some-thing and potentially—in the potential
details—something different. Different *what* is an opened
ended answer to the open ended question: different *how*?
that has to be—because it can only be—answered by you.

Which is to say, developmentally you are you: you are
your responses to human nature combined with your view
of what *you* think human nature is.

I think our human nature is an immutable albeit
identifiable something that we have to identify correctly in
order to survive and identify deeply in order to thrive.

By deeply I mean in the scientific sense of acquiring a
scientist's knowledge of our human nature.

If the *unexamined* life isn't worth living, then the *examined* one is worth it to a degree of ecstasy that is as high as is the examination deep.

Our development is all about being human and becoming human and vice versa—becoming human and being human.

And with one exception—for all living organisms including humans—being is before becoming.

The exception is in the womb where it's all about becoming—*becoming* a born, individual human *being*.

(And we can even notice the literalness of it all: becoming a human who is now being—voila! a born, individual, human … being … in the world as in: is exis(IN)tence, that is, an individual human being that *does* exist.)

(Since existence is *not* inside ~~ti(existence)~~me; time is inside exist(ime)ence, the concepts of being and becoming do not apply to existence in the same way; only the concept of being applies and this is why the correct answer to the question: Which came first, the [*everything that exists*] chicken or the [*every*] egg [*thing that comes from existence*]? is: the chicken.)

We are conceived; we become; we are born; we be.

A million seconds later we be something else, something more. Looking back at the time gap we say we became but while in the time gap we were becoming.

We were becoming more developed physically and mentally as same can be witnessed by parents and other adult human beings when they observe the growing and developing baby who is very very rapidly turning (via nature's automatic growth processes) him or herself into an infant. A growing and developing infant who learns how to crawl and eventually walk—and in the process—

transforming him or herself into a toddler who eventually also learns how to turn his or her babbles into meaningful words and eventually those words into complete thoughts and in the *process* transforming him or herself into a kid.

We now here now, as fully grown, adult selfishness seeker-saviors-of-our-own-soul persons, *are* interested in the mental—that is, the psycHological—parts of the growing and developing that human beings obviously do.

And that we, qua human beings, obviously did.

Our psycHological development—like our physical development—is a being *and* becoming and becoming and being *process.*

PsycHologically we are *dynamic* beings.

Since our psycHology develops over time we can think of it as an evolutionary process.

But with an important difference: evolution of living species takes millions of years and because of the large time spans involved the boundary conditions change so dramatically over time that the *process* is not repetitive in the same way *in the same place.* Evolution of our psycHology on the other hand takes millions of seconds and is repeated over and over and over again throughout the entire duration of our—relatively speaking—boundary-conditions-stable finite life.

Evolution of *species* is long and linear, of human psycHology, short and repetitive.

Or that is, evolution of our human psycHology is short and cyclical, albeit, still linear albeit with loops like the projected shadow onto a stationary white background of the traced out line of a button welded to the rim of the wheel-ing and dealing that we engage in as we roll down life's road.

This traced out line is like a string of uniformly spaced (k)nots or like a movie reel of individual time-lapsed still pictures of the kind before digital electronics when movies were printed on celluloid and wound up into a big wheel/reel and then replayed as a byproduct of unwinding it through a projector.

Imagine a piece of that string—or celluloid—to be 1 million seconds long. One million seconds = 11.574074074074074074074074074 = 11.57407 days = *about* a dozen days. So in *about* two weeks from now (or should I say, *about* squared) if you are closer to 24 months old than you are to 24 years old, *nature* will see-to-it that you will be *more* and *better* more. If however, you are closer to the 24 years then it is up to you via your nature given power of volition to see-to-this *self improvement* with the *capacity* to see-to-it growing from a *low* level when you *were* a toddler—that is, low albeit greater than the zero level at your birth instant—to its fully developed, 100% capacity *as fast as you can* grow it—*after*, that is, it has been *completely* unfolded by your human nature *as-a-capacity* **to be** developed and grown.

hgtikoi{{{Which is to say "we" *hypothesize*: H_0: the penultimate leg in our **full** psycHological development is *successfully* going from programmed-to-volitional **self regulation** *as fast as we can* with faster being *better* than slower.}}}

Life as a metaphysical force—we speculate further—harnesses the evolutionary *process* and makes it be a gazillion times faster.

Life in this sense *is* speed.

Though the time is drastically speeded up, the *process*, qua process, is the same; it involves steps (of some kind) even if we don't yet know what those kinds are.

Process is ordered steps completed over time so as to reach a pre-determined goal *in-a-timely* fashion.

Steps in this context are identifiable, concrete, sequential *events* wherein the occurrence of the next event depends on the already occurred previous event—i.e., learning how to walk was preceded by learning how to crawl and learning how to run was preceded by learning how to walk.

Running as process depends on walking which depends on crawling which depends on you choosing to move yourself away from point A and/or towards point B.

That is, immutable human nature has to use metaphysical *processes* (crawling-walking-running for example) as it is not at "liberty" so to speak to invent its own order. To my knowledge there is not one single recorded case of a new born human baby hitting the deck and *running* out the delivery room door tearing its umbilical cord asunder in the *process*, or, for that matter running *anywhere* until some time *later* in its *development*.

Physical development is a fact.

Physical development is a process.

In like fashion the psycHologically developed you now reading this book is thee "bundle of joy" that *you* personally have developed so far. A bundle of all *your* responses to human nature since the day you were born. A bundle of all of *your* TFAjot's (see Glossary).

A bundle of the responses that you personally made to your human nature—including the responses you made to what you think—right or wrong—human nature is.

Biocentric Psychology calls these psycHological responses your *personality* and even though selfishman wants to make his bundled responses work for his self—that is, work to get his *needs* met—selfishman is also interested in the wider view of personality that we call *personal identity*.

Personal identity is our actual personality integrated with our actual view of what we think we are—including, if any, those internal compartmentalized parts of ourselves that we don't know what to do with just yet. That is, we do know all of this about those compartments: "they" aren't being integrated and we suspect they can't be— metaphysically can't be—integrated because contradictory ideas can't be integrated and since we know integration is the hallmark of mental development and the capstone of all our psycHological efforts we just don't know *yet* what to do with "them".

hgtikoi{{{Later on—in some f.u.t.u.r.e book—we will discover that we need to know and understand BiO Spiritualism's **SVTOUL** theory in order to deal *properly* with our "compartmentalized" selfs.}}}

We commit to do something with them eventually—after first learning all we can about our personality and our personal identity.

Our *specific* personal identity is our *personal answers* to a whole bunch of questions.

Are we originally sinful?

No.

Are we automatically good?

No.

Can we be good?

Yes.

Can we be evil?

Yes.

Can we know?

Yes.

Are humans the source of the good?

Yes.

Are humans the source of the evil?

Yes.

Are we human?

Yes.

Should we give god credit for our good and blame ourselves for our bad?

No. We should give ourselves credit for our good and purge ourselves of our bad.

Do we have a conceptual capacity?

Yes.

Do we have the power to reason?

Yes.

Are we born with a college transcript and/or high school diploma attached to our name?

No.

How many cycles does it take to get to these educational degrees or their equivalent in learning this 'n that about the world?

That is, what's one way to partition our development into *time* intervals?

Birth-to-terrible two's plus or minus a year = 0 to 3

Second turn of the wheel = 3 to 6.

Third and fourth turns = 6 to 9 and 9 to 12 respectively.

Double this and we are at the fulcrum point—that is, 24 years of age—where we either continue swimming to **full** adulthood or sink into the quicksand of *internalizing* our particular culture's specific messages of self-sacrifice and self-immolation which are calibrated to herd us towards self-destruction and servitude to The Group. A self destruction that starts, as we've already noted (Chapter 1) with ego-destruction and it starts with those in our culture who want us destroyed for their own reasons—be it to control us for their own purposes or to prevent us from reminding them—by our very existence as self honoring humans—of the evil "they" have committed—committed either consciously or by **default**—against themselves.

The *process* of *defaulting* is x.

The *process* of *choosing* the evil over the good is y.

The *process* of *undoing* x **and** y is z.

That is, x, y and z are *unknown* quantities to be determined and filled in, in the f.u.t.u.r.e.

hgtikoi{{{It is not impossible to get stuck or otherwise be frozen as it were in one or more of the early development cycles along one or more of our psycHological dimensions for a long long time and if the **Biocentric Psychology** phrase, "... *a child walking around in an adult body...*" applies to you then you should consider looking into **your** position on the **role** *volition* does or does not play in-your-view of human life.}}}

If, after all of the above considerations you should find yourself (so to speak) in a psychotherapists office—that is, in the office-of-the-one *you* have *chosen* of your own *free will* to be the temporary scientist of you—you are want to be who you actually are and your therapist can want this too but he or she also wants you to be his or her theoretical view of what they think you *should* become.

hgtikoi{{{Some therapists know their "theoretical" view *explicitly* and some don't; still, they all have one—and as individuals they differ only in the methods they employ to get you where *they* want you to go. This is why you have to identify to the best of your ability, WHERE *you* want to end up before you enter therapy—e.g., I want to be *less* emotionally repressed and *more* emotionally expressive after therapy.}}}

And this is why it is important to have a thorough understanding of your own philosophy of life.

Even if–heaven forbid—you desire to be a serious contender among the world's social metaphysicians who—with their silent voices—clamor to become the world's best altruists.

We can observe—notwithstanding Dr. Nathaniel Branden's myth busting article, "*Isn't everyone selfish*" (see Glossary)—we can observe that even if you desire to be the world's "best" self**less** person you can't escape the fact that the *starting* desire for this is **you** *wanting* something **you** consider "good". And as **you** work to kill this "good" in you—as you *must* in order to achieve *your* goal to be *truly* selfless—I hope you don't succeed. I hope you don't succeed because self*less* people are the primary reason selfish people have not (yet) been able to establish a *sustainable moral* political-economic system here in the United States of America, let alone here on planet earth. That is, a truly free, 100% *ofc* political-economic system (*o* bjectivism *f* air *c* apitalistic system).

The other primary group responsible for this failure are those who are excessively low on the *authentic* self-esteem scale. And as if this weren't enough, since faith and (initiated) force do go hand-in-hand and self*less*ness as a way-of-being in the world depends on faith as the *means* to *justifying* it you will become a thug *in-the-process* of succeeding at being selfless and thereby be a *direct* physical threat to the rest of us.

The *degree* of your thuggery IN ACTION—stemming of course from the *degree* of your commitment-to-FAITH that you have *actually* dedicated your consciousness to—will depend on opportunity and circumstance. That is, on "opportunity" presented by others—e.g. the Hitler created "opportunity" for the brownshirts in pre World War II Nazi Germany *to be* Brownshirts. And individual circumstance for example as say someone *pushes you to **your** core* irrational, faith-based premises (rather than taking care *not* to do this *because* they are afraid of you) and you lash out at them, slapping or slugging them perhaps.

(Getting *angry* is a prerequisite to slugging and so getting angry *and* slugging go together but getting angry and ***not*** slugging—since as a human being you have the power of volition, that is, the power to not slug—is also a *possible*— read, ***reason*** based—outcome.)

Since the only "circumstance" that you have *direct control over* is in your *thinking* and since the only "opportunity" you want is the opportunity to be self responsible, it is *your* responsibility to NOT ***be*** a thug by NOT ***becoming*** one.

That is—as we already know—man *is* a *being* of self made soul.

Of course, psychotherapy isn't the only "controlled" environment for you to "test" your ideas of what's what against the facts of reality; you also can use your day-to-day life to throw in a test or two here 'n there as you are working to *become* who you want to be.

hgtikoi{{{ ...but be careful, don't forget the Ranger tower event from before ... that is, not all test ideas are good ideas simply because they are labeled "tests" ... }}}

(I want you to be **selfish**—that is, **virtuous**—so that I don't have to worry about you being easy fodder for the Professional Bureaucrats—that is, the Bureaucratic Mentality, that is, the BM's—who want to *control* you as t.h.e.i.r interim means of controlling all of us as t.h.e.i.r ultimate means of providing t.h.e.m and t.h.e.i.r's with an "identity" that they lack but desperately need. Since existence is identity, non-identity is nonexistence, hence, human beings need identity more than anything else. Some kind of identity is better than no kind. Since there are only two kinds of identity for humans: self or other, if T.H.E.Y *refuse to **own*** self, then other—group—identity is the only thing remaining to T.H.E.M as "other" has always been the source of their *sense* of "self" so that, **voila!** T.H.E.I.R mental soup is a hodgepodge of other-bodies and other souls to such a large degree that t.h.e.i.r entire mental universe is governed by one law: all that which is not-me is the good.)

Authentically selfish people cannot and will not be controlled by BM's or anyone else for that matter. Authentically selfishman is *autonomous* man and *authentically* autonomous man is Selfishman.

To this end then your total, complete *view* of *your* personal psycHology—that is, your *personal identity*—is like a works-in-progress (wip's) report on all the self-assertion *insertions* and all the self assertion *experiments* you have ever conducted over your entire lifespan up to this point in time—or at minimum, conducted since your last wips report.

And as you continue to *be* and to run more tests, you
gradually build up the *need* to write more interim as well
as *final* wip's reports.

Your final reports are called "integrations" and your
interim ones "progress reports" on "The Art and Science of
becoming and *being* and vice-versa"—*becoming*
selfishman and *being* selfishman and being selfishman and
becoming *more* selfish.

Hence, our earlier comment that selfishman's work is
never done is underscored here by a *psycHological
principle*: na(IN)ture, human beings are *being* and
becoming beings.

Conscious—i.e., volitional—self assertion experiments can
be assigned to the becoming parts.

And the key concept here is, "experiment".

In science, *experiment* is part and parcel of what is known
as *The Scientific Method.*

Selfishman AND *Aspiring* selfishmen love the scientific
method.

The scientific method is the method of **observing** reality,
thinking about these observations and forming hypothesis
about how reality works and then **testing** these hypothesis
in reality, gathering data from these experimental tests and
then **evaluating** the data by comparing it to our "theories"
about what the data *should* be and adjudicating any
discrepancies by refining our theory or our tests or both as
same is determined by our intelligence and our intellectual
integrity as guided by our unswerving desire to **match**
reality.

Reality, again per Objectivism and the *reality* of death—or
rather, vice versa—a**lways** *has the final say.*

The foregoing process description of the scientific method is the answer to the question, how do we wire our own brain so as to gain *correct* cognitive understanding of the universe in which we live?

Rather, it is a *description* of how we **SHOULD** so "wire".

Should that is *if* cognitive competence is our goal.

For example, in physics, or better yet, from my own *first hand* experience as a test engineer.

I conducted experiments in heat transfer (my engineering specialty back in the day) to discover the cooling effectiveness of water cooled flat plates attached to the back of heat generating printed circuit boards. In one such test I instrumented a flat copper plate assembly in one of my first ever out-of-college-into-the-real-world-of-work experiments by touching the bead of the thermocouples I was using to the surface of the plate so as to get a *pure* surface temperature. I of course knew all the appropriate theoretical relationships between temperature and heat flow and hence "knew" what I "should" get from the experimental results.

I did not get it.

My temperatures were low by a significant amount and at first I knew not why.

My first response was, jfk everything I learned in college was worthless.

This was then followed by, what's wrong? Did I miscalculate the amount of heat being pumped into the copper plate? is some of the heat going somewhere else? are my instruments measuring correctly? wtfigo? (though this last—what the f is going on?--was not part of *then* but is something I'm adding *now* as back *then* I didn't articulate my—then dwindling now growing—selfishness parts out loud like I do now).

So what the f *was* going on?

To make a long story short as it turns out one of the things "they" didn't teach me in college (or one of the things they taught some Monday morning when I stayed home from a hangover from the weakend and so failed to pick up on it) was that when measuring *surface* temperatures with thermocouples you need about a half inch or so of the lead *in addition to the bead* in contact with the surface else you'll get an average temperature between the hot surface and the surrounding cooler room air and not "pure" surface temperature.

I made the *adjustment*, reran the experiment and voila! IT WORKS IN THEORY *AND* IN PRACTICE as I got results that made sense given that all the input parameters were correct and my instruments—having been rechecked by me, e.g. I put all my thermocouples into an ice bath and low and behold they measured 32.5 degrees Fahrenheit, but now what the f ... water freezes at 32 °F so why isn't it this? and I then had to adjust for my *context* which meant for the effects of barometric pressure as my lab was not at sea level but higher up (800 to a 1000 feet here in middle Minnesota) and so on and so forth.

The scientific *method* works!

Our interest here of course is neither physics nor heat transfer per se but it is *us* per se—me per se in my case, you per se in yours—hence, The Scientific Method in real psychology is *each* of us:

> **observing** *our selfs* in reality, **thinking** about these observations and forming hypothesis about how we work in reality

and then ***testing*** these hypothesis *in reality*, gathering data from these experimental tests and evaluating the data by comparing it to our "theories" about what the data *should* be and adjudicating any discrepancies by refining our theory or our tests or both as same is determined by our intelligence and our intellectual honesty as guided by our unswerving desire to **match** reality.

(See my <u>Yes</u> book for examples, especially pages 71, 121, 194 (Foot Note 175) and 331.)

Like true scientists then, intelligence *and* intellectual honesty get added to our list of *cardinal* values. (You cannot have too much intelligence and you cannot have too much intellectual honesty.)

Since we now have *enough* **objective** cardinal values— *intellectual honesty, intelligence, self acceptance, authentic self esteem, health*—to get started towards achieving selfishman status we proceed towards finishing our psycHological work by focusing on becoming *autonomous* man.

＊ ＊ ＊ ＊ ＊ ＊ ＊ ＊ ＊ ＊ ＊ ＊ ＊ ＊ ＊ ＊ ＊ ＊ ＊

Chapter 6

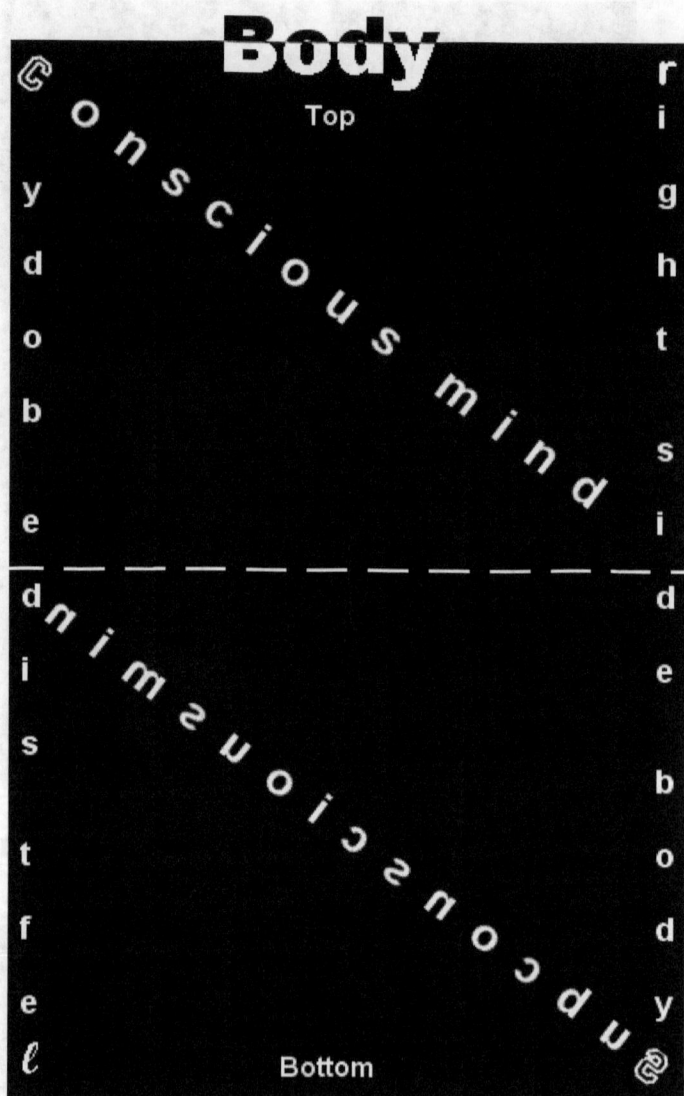

Your blank entries are your blackest sins.

you are here

volition

- - - - - - - - - -

automatic

what's in here

is for the slogging around

are the only one who

u ta find out,

to figure out as you

can do it

who's this?

Remember Ayn Rand, the world's *best* philosopher who argued (in Galt's Speech and elsewhere) that our blank entries are our blackest sins?

See Glossary for link to Galt's Speech which the following excerpt is from:

> "Thinking is man's only basic virtue, from which all the others proceed. And his basic vice, the source of all his evils, is that nameless act which all of you practice, but struggle never to admit: the act of blanking out, the willful suspension of one's consciousness, the refusal to think—not blindness, but the refusal to see; not ignorance, but the refusal to know. It is the act of unfocusing your mind and inducing an inner fog to escape the responsibility of judgment—on the unstated premise that a thing will not exist if only you refuse to identify it, that A will not be A so long as you do not pronounce the verdict 'It *is.*' Non-thinking is an act of annihilation, a wish to negate existence, an attempt to wipe out reality. But existence exists; reality is not to be wiped out, it will merely wipe out the wiper. By refusing to say 'It is,' you are refusing to say 'I am.' By suspending your judgment, you are negating your person. When a man declares: 'Who am I to know?'—he is declaring: 'Who am I to live?'

If this is so, *then* it logically follows: unblanking them, i.e., filling-them-in, must be our whitest virtues.

Well ... not exactly. *Not* blanking in the first place would be our whitest virtues.

Unblanking them is simply the price (in time currency) we have to pay to make ourselves *more* mentally healthy.

Mental health, remember, is *the unobstructed capacity for reality-bound cognitive functioning—and the exercise of this capacity* [Branden, *The Psychology of Self-Esteem*, Nash Publishing, Los Angeles, CA, 1969, p. 94, also see Glossary under Biocentric Psychology]. Since we can easily recognize that *maintaining* blankouts requires mental workarounds, that is, mental *detours*, which like their literal counterparts in the external world are *obstructions* in your path in that they cause one to use more time in addition to more gas and/or electricity when "driving" *to* a specific conclusion in one's own mental universe so that *blankouts* require more mental energy than is necessary.

Or stated differently, *eliminate* your blankouts, get more mental energy as a consequence.

More mental energy is good.

(All *action* requires work. All work is energy expended. Mental action is work. Mental action requires expending energy. What the associated energy units are we don't yet know—that is, mental energy spent could simply be a euphemism for "time spent". For now this *path*, this *direction* to figure this out will not be taken *because* it is beyond the scope of our present concerns.)

Blankouts are failing to draw a conclusion when you have the data to do so because the conclusion would wreak havoc with your innermost values—be it your core value, or any of the several values surrounding your core.

Technically speaking of course the blanking isn't just in regards to core values but since core values carry the most intensity—that is, the most *motivation* to "not" see if the seeing would be a serious challenge to the core—and because core values by definition are the most important values the blankouts involving core values are the ones we *should* be most concerned with. (Even if your particular hierarchy of values is upside down it doesn't matter, your core is *your* core and so you will be affected just like those of us who have a right side up value hierarchy that— although it might not *yet* be a perfect match to reality in *all* its values—it is—qua correct side up (e.g., selfish'ism at the top; self immolation at the bottom and on the verge of being purged out of the system forever)—it is *better than* an upside down one (i.e. take the preceding example and reverse it, that is, turn it upside down: self immolation at the top; selfish'ism at the bottom and on the verge of being purged out of the system forever).

So, depending on the degree of *your* courage and guts, go for the core sooner rather than later.

Life after all is finite and we don't have time to release the energy in each and every *single* neuron-to-neuron "bond" one such bond at a time as same are being maintained by us based on our *errors* and/or evasions.

Human beings *can* make errors—this is *half* of the meaning of the observation: *man is not omniscient.*

The other half is: Human beings *do* make errors.

Human beings can evade reality—this is *one* meaning of the idea: *man has volition.*

Another meaning is we have *control* over the workings of our own mind.

And still another is, Human beings can choose to face reality.

That is, facing reality is *better* than evading it.

Everybody knows this.

Don't they?

But of course the real question is, do you?

Do you face *reality* automatically or at least semi-automatically or do you do the opposite, evade reality automatically or semi-automatically.

That is, are you pretty *unobstructed* in your *reality* bound cognitive functioning or are you *obstructed*, blocked ... repressed?

One way to perform a simple little *experiment* with yourself as means testing your *introspective* and *unobstructed* (as opposed to your unselfaware and repressed) nature is to recast the above into the following and as you re-read it *pay attention to the inner you* and the *actions* of *your* mind.

> *Life after all is finite* and we don't have time to sweat the small stuff.
>
> So to speak.
>
> But of course, we *do* have time to sweat the big stuff.
>
> And that is what we *should* do—spend our time *efficiently*, not inefficiently.
>
> In our finite life we *shouldn't* waste time releasing an eye-dropper's worth of energy from an irrationality that says "all red haired women are hot headed" when we *could*, hence *should* spend that same time releasing a vat or two's worth of energy from the irrationality that says, "yes, there is a god and I accept that on *faith*".
>
> That is, to repeat, depending on the degree of your *courage* and guts go for the core *sooner* rather than later.

Another way to check out the degree—if any—of *your* repression—that is, *your* mind's automatic avoidance reaction to its own mental contents—is to launch a serious challenge to a core belief and observe yourself internally to see how your mind ricochets, that is, how "rick·oh·schay·eey" your mind is—or is not for that matter.

> That is, if you more or less can drive straight to your core giving your reality based reasons at every cross-roads along the way then the belief is more than likely rational and/or more or less rational and so pick a different one.

> If after trying several of these and you feel pretty clean and unobstructed, then welcome to the *land* of happiness. (Or at least to *half* of it, that is, to the *noncontradiction* part.)

> (But just-in-case you are rationalizing, place a *suggestion* in your mind as a standing order to alert your attention to any subconscious challenge that might be going on outside your focused awareness—be it in day-dreaming and/or night-dreaming.)

> That is, you are—metaphysically are— *responsible* for **_everything_** you think and say and *do* so why not accept this responsibility sooner rather than later.

Yes, I know, it is a rhetorical question.

But hey, *Save Yourself Brother*.

I had to and so do you.

* * * * * * * * * * * * * * * * * * * *

PART 2:

At the resurrection of your mind

"I am speaking at the resurrection of your mind, in the brightness of that light in which you are growing, ... The word that will save you is, 'selfishness."

—Gary Speak,
from Gary's parallel universe here,
December 31st, 2011, as the majority (76%+) of *his* blankouts have been filled in, in the here and now …
Now. Here.

Chapter 7

The new New Selfishness Training Institute

The *original* STI—having been jailed by The State—is *still* in jail, albeit, with its *parts* making jail breaks—not every day, but—in every book I write and publish.

The second, died-on-the-vine non-profit STI is inside *Gary's Venns* at *gdeering.com*. (reference: "GIVE ME SELFISHNESS OR GIVE ME DEATH", written, 12/31/97 and used as the seminal article in the launch of *gdeering.com* eight months later on August 30th, 1998. The article is posted under the **Philosophy Venn/STI** as an unexamined letter to be opened.)

The third and newest, albeit not final just newest STI—*The Selfish'ism Institute*—is **herein**. (That is, is essentially **this** book.)

The Selfish'ism Institute—as a concept—is really the *PsycHological Re-Training Institute* (PRTI) dedicated to helping you fill in your own blank(out)s.

If you require it.

Blanks, as pointed out in Chapter 6, are *man-made*. They are made by us blanking-out *by choice* rather than drawing *a logically valid* conclusion when we do in fact have enough *evidence* to so draw. For example: Bob died on Monday, Sally on Tuesday and Hal on Thursday, therefore, on Friday I conclude: *some people are mortal* or do I conclude, therefore, "some people live forever in the hereafter"? or do I conclude, *who can know anything, I don't know what to think.* The first of course is logically valid, the second not and the third is a *blank-out* created by the "concluder" in the "concluder's" own personal mental universe. So for such a "concluder" who has hundreds if not thousands or more of such blank-out "conclusions" in his or her personal mental universe—i.e., *particularized* consciousness; i.e. *mind*—traveling down such a mind's pathways in search of knowledge will probably be experienced as driving down an excessively potholed road – rat-ah-tat-tat-rat-ah-tat-tat one jaw-clenching-bumpidy-bump-bump-bump hole after another so that the person has to "change lanes" so to speak and/or "paths" so to speak and even change to such a degree that he or she has to change the direction of the search or simply *abandon* the search altogether because the bumpiness is simply too much for a (physical) body to endure.

So to speak.

Solution: Check your premises and *fill in the potholes*.

I am going to figure that if you have read this far you might have a few potholes of your own to fill in.

If you do this "pot-hole-filling-in" your *reward* is a smoother ride in search of knowledge (or we should really say, a smoother ride in the *inductive* part of *creating* knowledge—that is, the part that requires a complete enumeration of *your* mental contents as you search through them for consistencies and contradictions in relationship to the particular thing about **reality** that you are trying to learn and/or understand. That is, that you are trying to noncontradictorily *integrate* into the totality of your mental contents.)

hgti>koi{{{human beings, another of our **hypothesis** has it, *are* **born with** the **power** *of induction*, specifically the power of induction-by-complete enumeration *of our own mental contents—ever heard the cliché:* **search your own soul first?** It is this *innate* power that the professional philosophers can help us expand and improve on as we develop and mature in our—human—thinking capacity. That is, pigs can't fly but birds can. TIPCFBBC or stated **differently: That is, birds can't induct but humans can**. **TIBCIBHC**.}}}

Because I (still) don't want to spend the time getting permission from The State to practice PT (PsycHological Therapy) I can only help you here *indirectly*. At some point in the f.u.t.u.r.e—not withstanding my one failed attempt a few years back (Appendix A, FOF_2)—I may elect to pursue such permission, but for now, not.

Consequently, if you use my written—read *self help*—materials to "cure" yourself of *all* your "ills" you will have to learn how to help yourself *directly* before you will be able to achieve your final goal of complete and total happiness here on this earth while you actually live and breathe.

At the end of the day of course this is really what you have to do *independent* of my getting licensed or not. And even though I realize I would be more help to you if we could meet face to face this is just not going to be the case.

That is, to repeat, "Save Yourself Brother".

I had to and so do you, albeit, not just *from* Religion and Formal Secular Humanism but also *from* all non-objective philosophies as well as *from* all contemporary—that is, all *non*-biocentric—psychologies.

(**And to facilitate your self-saving, reference the following example of self-help help** *if* you want a works-in-progress *schematic* to follow as you work to develop yourself into a person who possesses *authentic* self esteem and then eventually into self-esteeming selfishman, then see the original STI's *Blue Brochure*, ©1993 (link FOF_3

Appendix A) which includes what back then was referred to as the RAISE™ Method —**R**ational **A**pproach to **I**ncreased **S**elf **E**steem: Self Esteem and SElfishness; reciprocally caused, spirally sought.)

I can't call my newest *Selfishness Training Institute* the PsycHological re-training institute because if I use the word *psychology* in such a way as to suggest that I *might* be a licensed psychologist, The State of Minnesota will throw me in jail (FOF$_1$). I am however, a *psycHologist* in the *scientist* sense of the term: *one who studies the attributes and characteristics that certain living organisms possess by virtue of being conscious organisms.* But I am not – and let me emphasize the NOT – a *licensed* **by** The State Psychologist.

I know it is true that this fact about me allows me to tout my superiority to those other licensed "psychologists" who *have* sold their soul to The State. However, to do so is to fall into the trap of *Social Metaphysics* with its comparison-to-others standard as the implicitly advocated *should be* standard for one's self esteem. That is, since SM is not good for you I am not going to succumb to the temptation to so engage.

Consequently, because of The State's all powerful thuggery I cannot—that is, I dare not—call my institute, "pretty" (that is, PRTI as in, **PsycHolo**gical **Re-T**raining **I**nstitute).

However, inside *our own soul* we can *make* our facts match reality rather than engage in euphemistic protectionism and hence properly label our own individual psycHological re-training "pretty" –that is, PRTI: *PsycHological Re-Training of the I*—and not have to fear Bureaucrats coming after us so to speak with a vengeance so to speak hell bent on killing our ego so to speak so as to make us more controllable so to speak.

That is, s*(IN)*ide *our own soul we can do* whatever we want and t.h.e.y can't stop us.

Well ... that's not *exactly* true, "t.h.e.y" – as in, *T.H.E.Y is the name* of those Ayn Rand *collectivists* in our *own* soul—those "they" (what we will later call Social Metaphysicians or SM's for short) can, but we are not going to let t.h.e.m. We are going to use our own *courage* and strength of conviction (that Selfishness *is* a virtue) to defeat them.

So, do yourself a favor and start your own re-training today. And remember: until and unless you achieve *being* selfish as reason & logic direct you *to be*, you cannot be happy.

Veni. Vidi. Vici. That is:

I came. (to the philosophical battle)

I saw. (what had to be seen)

I conquered. (my own errors)

That is:

ego faustum;

I *am* happy;

et potest etiam;

and you can be too. [1]

---

[1] I am aware that relying on my one (now ancient) high school Latin class plus the google translator for my "Latin" is risky. But it is the *sentiment* that needs to be grasped: the battle for your mind is just that—*a battle*—and whether

you win that battle or loose it is entirely, 100%/completely up to you—ad victor, happiness.

Chapter 8

Selfishness Training vs. (BiO) Spiritualism

* * *

The Selfishness Training Institute, f.u.t.u.r.e
*where your rehab FROM sacrificing yourself—BACK
TO—saving yourself can begin*

1. You are born selfish human, albeit, *embryonic* in the *self*
sense as same is described by the starting concept ego and
100% selfish in the physiological sense of physical
systems dedicated to one and only one thing: the continued
physical existence of the conscious-biological unit known
as, [insert your name here].

2. By **Nature** *you are selfish* for the majority of your first
decade of life.

3. If you are now an adult and NOT selfish then something
bad and/or some bad things happened between *then* and
now.

4. The latest **STI** iteration: *The Selfishness Training
Institute, f.u.t.u.r.e* – via all its previous and new and
developing processes aimed at helping you become your
own savior – might be your last salvation.

....

5. *Yes*, *salvation*—as in a saving or being saved;
preservation from destruction—is the correct word; that is,
preservation from *continued* **self** destruction is the correct

concept. In a *free* society—excluding murder—there is no other kind.

....

BiO Spiritualism.com, ETC.
*where your **habituation** from selfish human-to-happy human can **continue***

1. *Develop-mentally* we transition from *programmed* self regulation to *volitional* self regulation somewhere between the ages of 9 and 39, with some of us closer to the 9 and others of us to the 39.

(I, the now 65 year old me, *started-the-transition-at-age-12* myself, did the *penultimate* leg between age 29 and 33 and completed the *final* leg before age 56. I speculate that it is possible for true geniuses—those with intelligence that *is* off the charts on the high side—to transition at ages below nine just as those at the opposite end of the spectrum, below-the-charts intelligence, can take significantly longer, going beyond age 75 to accomplish it. And it seems logical to conclude that *some* people—of intelligence levels over the entire spectrum—*never* make the transition because its start *and* its completion requires exercising one's human power of volition—a *power* that has only *one* non-trivial prerequisite: you have to be a human being to have it and qua human you have to **_choose_** to exercise it. That is, you have to use your nature given power of volition to exercise your nature given power of volition . This single fact is what makes understanding *volition-as-a-power* difficult. That is, after the fashion of the observation that *ego* is '*the only bird that can support its own cage*', (Victor Hugo, *Les Misérables*) we have the (internally) observable fact that: *volition* is *the only light that can turn itself on.* And in the all of the known universe *volition* exists in one and *only* one place: *inside the soul of man*.)

2. Since it is a process, the transition from programmed-to-volitional self regulation can be completed to varying degrees of success ranging from half (assed) to full-and-complete.

(For short hand purposes we can think of the transition from programmed-to-volitional self regulation as going from child volition, which is *the only light that **can** turn itself on*, to adult volition, which is *the only light that **has** to turn itself on*.)

And a complete transition means, 100% completed which according to my speculation based on my own personal experience, is doable via the "trip-wire threshold" of 76%-and-rapidly-increasing-towards-the-100% completed transition.

100% completed, or simply *completed* has a starting point and that point starts with 3 out of 4 new trials where our proactive choices are chosen over our reactive responses. When we learn a new, better way to do something (sports training from your own sports interests can be used here as example) and we do it a minimum of 3 out of 4 times the opportunity-to-do-it arises and we notice that it is better (be it a golf swing or jump shot or treating one's *self* seriously that *is* better) than the 1 out of 4 times that we still use the old method we then get excited. Then after 6 such successful sets of the new behavior (this is the speculation part based on a psycHHological science I haven't fully developed yet called—not psychometrics, but—teleömetrics) or that is, in 18 out of 24 opportunities or 75% of the time we can and do change to the new normal from the old one so that when we do the 18th +1 out of the 24th +1 = 19/25 = 76% we start the rapid rise to "completion". That is, after the 76% threshold the old way isn't even used, isn't done, isn't tried anymore as it is a waste of time compared to the new, better, improved way and so over the same frequency interval where we did 3 new implementations before we now do 4 instead. By the nature of numbers we are increasing by 33% the rate we transition to the new way. And so we end up completing the transition to the new normal and by completed it means **100% of the time** going forward **we do** ... **we use** ... **we implement** the new way and 0% of the time, that is, we **never** use the old way. Then in the f.u.t.u.r.e —that is, in our personal future—when we slip back to the old way once out of a 1000 times or so it allows us to enjoy the cliché, 'never say never', but if we slip significantly more it helps us understand where the biblical metaphor about the fall from grace came from—i.e., from human not heavenly experience. ... i.e., old habits die hard and such is the human condition.)

hgtikoi{{{many, if not all, *kgv* (see Glossary) biblical images and vignettes are metaphors for the many enduring qualities of the human condition and since primitive man, qua man, had a **need** for philosophy just as does modern man, he, primitive man, had to do the best he could to develop a philosophy—that is, a metaphysic, a epistemology and a ethic—to meet his human *need* for one. Since *Objectivism* hadn't been discovered **and** developed yet, primitive man **invented** Religion.}}}

3. If you are older than the midpoint of the programmed-to-volitional self regulation transition – that is, if you are more than 24 years old — and have not yet started this transition then you are in psycHological trouble.

4. Go back to STI and when you feel comfortable *choosing* your lots in life you are ready for *BiO Spiritualism* and its focus on helping you attain *true happiness* here on this

earth while you actually live and breathe. (If you need more detailed help in managing the transition to full volitional self regulation refer to and use the original **STI Counseling Services** *Blue Brochure* (FOF₃) that contains a schematic—or as I like to call it, a treasure map—on how to make your way through the transition zone to all the many treasures on the selfishness side.)

....

5. **<u>Yes</u>**, *happiness*—as in the Ayn Rand definition of same: *a state of non-contradictory joy, a joy without penalty or guilt, a joy that does not clash with any of your values and does not work for your own destruction*—is the correct word; that is, happiness as a psycHological state of your own S*elfMadeMan* making is the correct *concept*. In any society that draws a sharp distinction between noncontradiction and self-consistency—that is, *all* noncontradiction is self-consistent but *not* all self-consistent is noncontradictory—there is no room for self delusion in answering the question about happiness: that is, *Am I happy?* In societies that don't draw distinctions no happiness is possible—be it of the muted, self-consistency type or of the *authentic*, free-flowing, noncontradictory kind.

....

✳ ✳ ✳

Selfishness Training is all about self-valuing.

BiO Spiritualism is all about self-caring.

You can't care about that which you don't value and you don't value that which you have been taught since time immemorial is valueless.

If you are a person who ___ ... has accepted the cultural
bromides against selfishness—especially the more serious
ones that want you to believe selfishness is evil—and as a
consequence you have worked overtime burning the
midnight gray matter to bury your self deep inside your
own psycHology then you have some back breaking
unearthing work to do.

Since human beings are strong you will be able to do the
work.

So I suggest you get started now rather than later shoveling
the bullstuff off of *you*.

Because, as I've asserted elsewhere in regards to these
matters: sooner *is* better than later.

Chapter 9

Resurrection

I am the kind of person who ____ ...

... had to resurrect his own ego.

Resurrect in this sense is a *measurement* concept.

It is a measure of *how much* **I** had *disowned* my own self.

It is a measure of how far I had gone down the religious road to self immolation and self sacrifice.

Self sacrifice—qua the moral ideal in Religion that it is—is the roadbed of self denial; self denial is the paved over roadbed leading to self disowning.

Self disowning terminates in the misery of disvaluing the self, which in its penultimate form is self repudiation and its *ultimate*, hellish form: **self rejection**.

Self rejection, self repudiation, self disvaluing—when done in reverse order—describes the *process* and ultimate end game of self *disowning* and it is *not* natural. Self rejection is a man-made, not nature made "value".

And since the *road to hell* – to quote a Religious sentiment – *is* paved with good intentions, and self sacrificing is good intention, where does this lead us?

If we are determined to *not* blankout any longer (see Chapter 6) it leads us to this inescapable conclusion: In Religion—Religion formal, Religion professional, Religion serious—*all roads lead to hell.*

But since religion doesn't have a monopoly on paved over, pockmarked, potholed psychoepistemological roadbeds it doesn't follow that religious people are the *only* ones who end up in the hellish psycHHological state of self rejection. (Nor does it preclude some religious people from escaping the self rejection fate but it does preclude calling this escape true happiness—unless of course such an escape is accompanied with a total and complete … X … that is … X_1 of three critical factors for religious people to accomplish before they can become truly happy. X_1, X_2, and X_3 are to be revealed in the f.u.t.u.r.e—reference doorsign.biz FAST TRACK TO HAPPINESS June 28, 2012 Newsletter for more).

Others (e.g., *Social Metaphysicians*—that is, those who choose to "see" reality **not** through their own eyes but through the eyes of others, be those others literal others— i.e. those who think such 'n such is true or false BECAUSE so 'n so says so—e.g., it is true BECAUSE Ayn Rand says so ...or be they sacred books—e.g., such 'n such is true or false BECAUSE the bible tells me so ... and so on ...) can and do too end up in the hellish psycHHological state of self rejection. (For more on *Social Metaphysics* follow **one** of *my* concretized mental paths:

gdeering.com→ *Gary's Venns* →
Guest→**psycho-epistemology**→teleömeter:)

But what others do do or don't do in regard to their own personal ego has no bearing on the depth to which we personally can bury our own individual one. (In all honesty even though I did bury mine, I didn't bury it *that* deep since I could always see its back so to speak -- like that of a partially buried rock — at the surface of the ground. By "see" here, I mean in my nightmares of yesteryear where I dreamt that I and others of my friends had "killed" *somebody* and buried the body *somewhere* and we were *now* in **danger** of being discovered by the authorities. (More on dreams and relaxation generated mental content later. Content such as that generated in one of Dr. Branden's Intensives—circa the first part of the second half of the last century—where he had us do deep relaxation exercises and then go into the psycho-therapy exercise of envisioning your own tombstone. In my personal response to this I envisioned my tombstone in the night time in the predawn dark where, in a flash of lightning I saw the epitaph that was printed thereon. Mine read, **Gary D. Deering / He is dead**. And *Yes*, the "is" was underlined in the stone.)).

If, however, the road to hell *is* paved with good intentions, and self sacrificing is good intention then *all* philosophies—primitive or modern—that preach and promote self sacrificing as the highest or in the very least a *very* high moral ideal, lead to hell.

Metaphorically speaking of course.

As long as you stay on this side of the abyss – the abyss of insanity that is.

Insanity, I surmise, must be the real hell. Since there isn't a literal hell—a hell of fire and brimstone of the bibles with an alive devil and all that Religion's religious metaphysics conjures up for its followers—it doesn't follow that there isn't a metaphorical hell accompanied with *real* wailing and gnashing of teeth. (For a first hand view of "wailing & gnashing" examples join and become a participant in a good psycho-therapy group—that is, one that deals with *serious* psycHological issues relating to personal motivation, including the lack thereof and psychoepistemology, including *both* the healthy kind and the f'd up kind.)

The wailing and gnashing of teeth is the "payne"—the psychic pain—one experiences from a life time of self

74

Selfish'ism

disowning that has summed to a large enough pile to bury
the ego-self beneath layers and layers of a psychic
ground—that is, dirt—that is so infested with snaky
"reasoning" processes that one cannot step or go
anywhere—introspectively speaking—without the little
bastards creeping one out as they threaten to wrap
themselves around ones psychoepistemological ankles and
make it so sloggingly difficult to walk – epistemologically
speaking – that one must decide that the snarky-snakes
have to go before a renewed sense of self—a self re-
owning—can even begin to take place. (If you are the kind
of person who has mastered the art – usually out of
necessity – of using the dream cycle part of the sleep cycle
to undo complex psychoepistemological *errors* from your
past you can usually recover fairly quickly from these
errors. That is, for those of us who are accomplished
dreamers in the psycHological sense of being able to use
this time of the sleep cycle to locate and cut
snaky/snarky/snarling "reasoning" paths in half and watch
them dissipate and die—i.e., disappear—and do so en
masse, makes this "problem" a fairly rapid, correctable
one. If, however, you are the kind of person who _____ ...
is trying to undo your irrational "neuronal nets" one-
neuron-at a time—e.g., through life-coaching rather than
psycho-therapy or through continued psycho-therapy by
others after you have depleted all that those others can
actually deliver rather than psycHHological-therapy by
self—you may not have enough life left to accomplish the
task. You especially may not have enough left if you spent
more than half of your life so far creating/making/
maintaining irrational neuronal net works—that is, ones
that go beyond simply NOT matching reality but into
CONTRADICTING it. (Given that there is no medical
reason – see Medical Doctor Guest on The Johnny Carson
TV Show circa 1970's or '80's — that our bodies can't last

at least a 150 years, the "more than half" of your life starts at age 76. So that if you are 76 and are indeed in psycHological trouble of the failure to transition kind then you simply have to decide to try and live to be a 152. Perhaps an impossible task, but nonetheless, one that gives you the room to try and complete the transition to volitional self regulation with its concomitant rIse to the higher happiness ledges as you join in the search and rescue mission that all humans can – metaphysically can – enjoy: the search for and rescue of true happiness.)).

Ultimately the "neuronal net changing" is a matter of mathematics and to give you a taste of this for our future work on it watch the French movie *Amélie* (Miramax Zoe Films, 2001) and the scene about half way into the movie where a guy is sitting on a park bench reading a magazine, slouched in a kind of funk. His funk as the subtitles' caption captures is that he is just learning there are more links in his brain than atoms in the Universe. By any reckoning—given that the number of ink atoms in the period at the end of this sentence is greater than 10 bazillion—the number of neuronal interconnect possibilities (links) in our brains is a really big number. Since contradictory ideas are held internally in some form as are irrational defenses and many other internal thingy's—things 2—it isn't that much of a stretch to envision the irrationalities that we do in fact hold, to consist of thousands if not millions and even possibly billions of interconnected neuronal pathways—all snarled up like a bad hairdo on a bad hair day—and that our attempt to straighten out a messy psycHology by untangling our hair as if it were a snarled fishing line—that is one hair at a time—is going to take a really long time. Why not use a comb and brush instead? The comb is STI—original plus all iterations—and the brush is BiO Spiritualism with the comber and brusher being formal

Objectivism and formal Biocentric Psychology or vice versa depending on psychoepistemological need as the omniscient know it alls watching—i.e. combing and brushing—over our left shoulder in our managed-by-us dream cycles (or right shoulder depending on your internal bias for right or left handedness) and/or upon awaking being our applied by us principles in living every moment in our awake life.

Self-rejection as metaphorical hell accompanied with real, psychic pain, is also a measurement concept. It is a measure of how badly we have f'd up our own psychoepistemology.

Psychoepistemology is our own *personal* thinking M.O. and how same is used by us to *validate* our own knowledge and values. It involves the relationship between our conscious, volitional, goal setting operations of mind and the automatic carry-outer functions of our subconscious mind. (For one very simple example of a psychoepistemological practice that is NOT mine but might be yours is to actually conclude that: "the enemy of my enemy is my friend", so that if this is you then it becomes part of your thinking modus operandi when it comes time for you to decide who is, is not your friend.)

The conscious mind, to repeat, sets goals, the subconscious mind meets them, the linking and stitching and back-n-forthing that goes on between them is part 'n parcel of our psychoepistemology.

Psychoepistemology is the software of the mind—*our* **psychoepistemology** is the software of *our* mind.

Psychoepistemology is about our *actual* thinking M.O. and how we as **individual** humans use our own, personal brain and central nervous system as the software scaffolding to manage the complexity of being a surviving and thriving, healthy, happy human being.

(The entire *rest of our body*—as the final, all inclusive 3rd part in **addition** to the *brain* part and *central-nervous-system* part of biological-physical man—is used, I speculate, by our *particularized* consciousness—that is, our specific, particular mind—to store the essence of every-single-thing streamed from-without-into-us and from-within-into-us in such a fashion that we have access to it all, albeit, in a kind of "as required/need to know" basis-way. That is, as required by us via our personally chosen queries—including old standing orders perhaps that "say"—albeit *erroneously*, but that *still* say—we don't need to know our false premises—as we struggle to solve all the problems of life that require solving in order for us as individuals to continue the healthy-happy, surviving-thriving human life process.)

(The "software" part of ourselves is our *actual* philosophy of life—a philosophy that is made up of an *actual* metaphysic, an *actual* epistemology and an *actual* ethic. The brain's neuronal networking capabilities is to our "software" what punched cards were to the early Main Frame Computers and what code lines in any *concrete* form that are readable by modern day computer processors are to today's computers. The language we use to write our software is literally our language—be it english, french, spanish, german, russian, etc. And internally we create all our own punched cards as it were by simply engaging in the many Self functions: **TFAjot**; that is, Thinking, Feeling, Acting, judging, observing, testing; that is, by being in the world; that is, by observing the world, theorizing about it, testing our theories and modifying our theories as required to **match** reality and then repeating the cycle and moving on to new interests after we have learned all we can or are interested in, in regards to some, one particular thing. For example, when I was 9 or 10 years old in fourth or fifth grade it was absolutely of the utmost interest and excitement to me to *discover* that by measuring the shadow of a yardstick and the shadow of a very tall telephone pole that through proportions I could determine the *real, actual* height of the telephone pole without having to actually climb it and actually measure it!!! Now of course—some half century later after a lot of been-there-done-that's—if I went outside and did this one, particular thing it would be a bit boring.)

For another example; if through a lifetime of language development and internal programming *dedicated* to self denial, self immolation, self sacrificing, self denunciation, self disowning, we have convinced our self that we were doing the right thing, perhaps it is time to re-evaluate our concept of "right".

So, if you too need to resurrect your own ego then use this chapter as your reminder to do it and get started at it as soon as you can.

Sooner is better than later.

If 76% or more of your own personal ego has been buried within your own psycHology then I suggest you start with any psychotherapy—life coaching will not work—that recognizes the value of self even if it may not yet recognize the value of selfishness. (Hint: In your search for a good psychotherapist look for the usage in their advertisements and/or intake meetings of the euphemistic phrases: rational self-interest, enlightened self-interest, self esteem and other substitutes for the Ideal that says, *Selfishness is a virtue*.)

Viewing Selfishness as a value, as a virtue is—ultimately—up to you—not your therapist.

If you buried less than 24% of your self and/or have successfully unearthed more than 76% of your disowned self, then to see what lays ahead visit all things BiO Spiritualist: BiOspiritualism.com; *Yes. (Is BiO Spiritualism the answer?)* on amazon.com and other gdeering.com web content and also continue on here.

Chapter 10

Re-I-ntegration

Reintegration of the " I " – that is, Re-I-ntegration — starts with a psycHological experiment.

Breathe and relax.

And breathe and relax some more.

When you are in a meditative relaxed state imagine yourself out in the country leisurely walking down a country road.

As you walk along you see the trees and green grass, smell the country's fresh air as it blows ever so softly through the trees on its way to somewhere down the road.

You notice what looks like a person standing by one of the larger trees located quite a ways ahead of you.

You continue walking at the same leisurely pace, knowing that eventually you will make it to that person and then you will be able to identify who it is.

Halt. Stop. Pause...

If you want to do this *experiment* read the above into an audio recording and then find a quiet, private place to do the *experiment* by listening to the recording and taking it one step further by continuing down the road and discovering *who* the person is that is standing by that tree.

I did the above *exercise* at a Branden Intensive almost a quarter of a century ago and it is in my mind as if it happened yesterday.

(See myCountryRoadExercise in the Glossary for more elaboration including prompting by our psychotherapist as means to helping us get the purpose of the exercise. You might want to wait until after you've tried the above as psycHological *experiment*, then read the Glossary item and redo it as psycHological *exercise*.)

I can't guarantee this exercise will help you in the same way it did me but I can guarantee that if you search for and *experiment* psycHologically—while holding on for dear life to Objectivism's three axiomatic concepts: *existence* exists, *consciousness* is conscious, and *A is A*—you *will* find the exercises that do help you out in your *renewal* quest and as such you eventually will achieve happiness and/or happIERness. You will, that is, if you don't die prematurely, that is, *before* the **greater** of these two probabilities: (1) before the life insurance actuary tables predict you will OR (2) *before* an age that is equal to or greater by at least 10 years than that of your oldest parent. (For me this means premature is before age 107 – which means in two more years I will have 40 more years to live, geez, I wonder, maybe I should go back to school and get my Ph. D in psychhology?; that is, maybe I will, but then again, maybe not ... I don't know, tbd.)

Re-I-ntegration means ego reintegration with the self and self with the ego.

Ego reintegration presupposes ego disintegration—to some degree; more or less, but not to no degree.

You'll know that you have achieved ego and self reintegration when you *experience **first hand*** this *unshakable* truth within your own self:

> *I have met the friend and he is I.*

Chapter 11

BiO Spiritualism's 3 P's revisited

I *have* met the friend and he *is* I.

So now what?

Spiritualism's 3rd and final of the 3 P's is the next step.

It is the **P***ersonal* heaven on earth that we are heading for.

Heaven On Earth is a mental state, the one we call, Happiness.

Heaven On Earth—*unlike* Religion's mystical version of heaven—has stops along the way. That is, in the Heaven On Earth version of heaven, happiness exists in degrees and these degrees are represented by plateaus.

There is of course a minimal degree and it is the 51/49 percent line. (Whether or not this "line" is a "product" of the degree of our noncontradictions AND our pro-joy stance or simply a combination of them is beyond our current scope – that is, I don't yet know which it is. *But this I do know*: if I live long enough, *the engineer in me will figure it out*.)

Nonetheless, for *starting* purposes, we are going to argue that if the totality of our mental contents and our mental action in regard to those contents is noncontradictory to a degree that is high enough so that when it is coupled with the degree of our *actual* pro-joy attitude that the product of the two is equal to 51% then we are at level one or plateau one of happiness.

After this, the sky's the limit. (With the concept of "sky" – perhaps, s.k.y? – a to be determined one.)

Your *continued* spiritualism then is to *increase* the degree of your noncontradiction and joy towards the 100% level and along with it by fact of physics decrease your degree of contradiction and misery towards the 0% level. (100% is both a metaphysical limit and a metaphysical *maximum*. For more see **Yes's**, Chapter 1.)

Notice how your growth towards *authentic* happiness via happIERness is a double whammy on the upside — when you increase the good you decrease the bad *as a byproduct* and so the good/positive forces are more and more and the bad/negative ones less and less so that the combined net force raIsing you up is *amplified*.

(And though we don't want to dwell on it, the reverse is obviously true – spiraling downward is the consequence of shunning the selfishness ethic and embracing the altruistic ethic – that is, the *others before self* as the *should be* standard for your moral choices.)

Your choice.

My choice.

Our choice.

What is?

All of the 3 P's are.

That is, all of the 3 P's *in the abstract*: **P**hilosophy, **P**sycHolo**g**y and the **P**ersonal:

> *Philosophy* is WHITE or **BLACK**, *PsycHology* is WHITE and **BLACK**, and spiritualism is the color of your *Personal* rainbow

> which equals:

All of the 3 P's *in the concrete*: Objectivism, Biocentric Psychology and Spiritualism.

BiO Spiritualism is *my* name for the Personal/Spiritual part so if you don't like my name for it insert your name for it or no-name for it beyond *Spiritualism* should be ok too:

> *Objectivism* is **LIFE** or **DEATH**, *PsycHology* is **PLEASURE** and **PAIN**, and Spiritualism is the color of your *Personal* rainbow application of all your conscious and subconscious *Objectivist* and *Biocentric* principles on a day-in-and-day-out interaction with all your *Personal* observations—including the one based on a *lifetime* of *introspective* observations *of* me, *by* me that is posited below in the form of a Q&A *to* me.

Q: Are yu the kind of person who is not a genius but yet smart enough to figure out that *Objectivism* and *Biocentric psychology* are the *best* of their kind and though you are not a person who demands the best in everything, when it comes to *philosophy* and *psycHology*, nothing but the best is good enough for yu?

A: <u>**Yes**</u>.

Epilogue

Too many people have erroneously accepted their culture's programming that *selfishness* is not only not a *virtue* but it is a *vice* of such high degree that a person is morally justified in concluding that "selfishness is evil". Consequently, we dare not exit our topic without dealing to some degree with *evil* as a "thing".

Heralding back to our beginnings here we can suggest that the most common response—both *Philosophical* and Religious—to this book's save yourself call-to-action is:

Save yourself from what?

The Religionist's answer is:

From evil.

The Philosopher's answer is:

From evil.

Both the Religionist and the Philosopher can share—and many do share—the view that evil is the *absence* of the good.

The problem is that the Religionist and the Philosopher can have—and many do have—*definitions* of the *good* that repel each other towards opposite ends of the spectrum.

If you as an adult—in the whole of *your* lifetime of experiences—have *failed* to discover the underlying *differences* between these two evil's—that is, between the *true* bad, the *true* evil (beneath the *ultimate* Evil) and the *false* evils—then hopefully this book will have helped you do so or at minimum it will have helped you get started in the right direction (i.e., The Philosophy of Objectivism) for doing so.

The falsest of evils—the antichrist of evils so to speak—is to turn *true* evil upside down and label *it* the good: e.g. the "good" is that which is *against* this life here on earth and the "evil" is that which is *for* it.

(Developmentally there are some steps missing in the foregoing but my need here is to cut-to-the-chase not detail it.)

Once this *reversal* is made by a human being, that human—and anybody else who happens to have the misfortune of coming in contact with it—is in danger with a capital **D**.

(That is, evil of type **D? D**angerous? … **D** - evil? … jfk … Devil!?!?!?!?!?!? … no-way hoe-zay … this is just coincidence … I think).

Don't be that upside-down human.

I say this more out of fear than out of knowledge.

I personally know of no one who has redeemed their self from ultimate evil, that is, from evil with a capital E.

Hence, I *fear* such is *not* metaphysically possible.

True ultimate evil (Evil) has to involve *actual* murder by an actual adult somewhere (e.g. Ted Bundy) or somehow (e.g. Charles Manson) or it isn't true evil—or rather I should say, it isn't *yet* evil with a capital E. In my whole life I personally only met one murderer and I didn't know the person long enough to see if they changed. Nor for that matter did I really know for sure if this person was a true murderer or not. It was said by a fellow therapist that this particular adult person was convicted of murder and I had no reason to doubt it.

That is, for now, for me, my answer to the *fundamental* question: *Can Evil redeem itself?* is:

No.

Therefore do not—and I repeat, do *not*—cross over the line separating bad/evil-from-Evil. The best way of course to not cross the e/Evil line is to *properly* define the good (see Glossary) and then honor it, praise it —*pursue* it.

And also do not forget to *properly* define the *evil*—the *absence* of the [properly defined] good—and then dishonor it, *damn* it—DON'T pursue it.

And we have to pause and note here that of the two definitions the most important one is the definition of the good (see Glossary).

Then with the *proper* definition of the good under our belt we can conclude that the mantra: *judge and be prepared to be judged* is the mantra of the courageous definer.

For example, if we look at all the murderers over the past fifty years or so—be they mass, serial or singular—surely we can conclude that if not all of them then for sure *some* of them must have at some point in their development crossed over the good | bad **line** by *preferring* the bad hence **choosing** *the bad* over *the good* and that is *why* they *eventually* crossed over the *good* || *evil* **divide** and **ultimately** ended up being murderers.

Evil—notwithstanding an Ayn Rand *Atlas Shrugged* quote: "A viler evil than to murder a man, is to sell him suicide as an act of virtue.", that is, in spite of this quote, I hold that evil with a capital E—is the *ultimate* evil and it has to entail murder which is the *ultimate* end point for those who justify to themselves that it is *right* (i.e., moral) to use *initiated* physical force to get their way. (See the Nazi's with their 'might makes right' "principle". A "principle" that makes the Nazi's the ugly case example of the *evil of initiated physical force*.)

Since the philosophical me *knows*—that is, *I see what I see and I know what I know* and I know—that the road to evil is paved with the "good" intention called the "Creed of Self-Sacrifice" so that I also know that to be *Self Responsible* means do **not** succumb to self-sacrificing, self-immolation, self-rejection Creeds.

To succumb or not to succumb, that is the question.

(And of course the correct answer is: *Don't.*)

And so to repeat from our beginnings here: at the end of the day we are each responsible for our self; no one can take this fact away from us.

Nor should we want them to.

To selfish man, the fact of self responsibility is reason to rejoice.

To make the connection that *by nature* we are self responsible is gloriously good news because one thing we know for absolute sure about (mother) nature is that she doesn't do *anything* half way. If nature demands self responsibility of us then nature gives us all the tools we need to achieve a state of full and complete self responsibility.

Our job is to achieve it.

I did my job.

It is now up to *you* to do *yours*.

Gary Dean Deering, Author
2009-2013

PS
Is spiritual murder prerequisite for existential murder?

Yes.

That is, yes *if* by spiritual murder you mean the *ultimate*, the end point, the maximum in degree of *self-disowning*—which, mathematically, is: *self rejection* + 1.

Is spiritual murder the necessary and sufficient condition?

No.

Spiritual murder AND an at-large cultural moral code *sanctioning* spiritual murder AND a Z-factor are the *necessary* and *sufficient* causes of evil.

Based on what I know today I conclude that the **Z-factor** is: a *being* that *volitionally* chooses its actions and except for the *one* exception of being **physically forced** to do something against its will it does **NOT** act unless it thinks it is *right*. With its view of what is *right* and *wrong* coming from its volitionally accepted code of a handful of values—that is, tucked away in the *core* of its being that we call its *soul* are a handful of values—it classifies as the *good* along with the logical-metaphysical consequence: *empty core, empty bag, empty/vacuous soul*—that is, the **absence** of *the good*—is *the evil*.

Such a Core Code—*volitionally* accepted **or** volitionally *allowed* to be absorbed from the at-large culture—we call a person's Moral Code.

Consequently I conclude: the cause of *all* evil—including the kind with a capital E—is the upside-down human with an inside-out soul on the prowl for its first victim.

And of course I also conclude: the cause of *all* good—including the kind with a capital G—is the up'*right* human with a *right'*eous soul on its journey to discover its next higher level of happiness.

And one final question: what is the *good* with a capital G?

Answer: stay tuned.

hgtikoi{{{If in your mind **you** are thinking the answer is
G od notice that by a *similar* process **I** could have thought
G ary and let me tell you that neither of these "answers" is
the correct **One**.}}}

FPS

So.

Make no mistake about it.

If you don't ***own*** Selfishness self-less-ness will own you.

A body without a self is a zombie.

A body with a *selfish soul* is an *individual* human being.

Appendix A
FOF$_n$
FACTS On File

FOF$_1$
(circa 1990)

The State of Minnesota trying to physically force me to give *them* credit for *my* ideas on psychology by *threatening* to put me in jail because I referred to my self, qua Founder *of* and Counselor *for The Selfishness Training Institute* as offering *psychological* counseling services and since I was not a licensed psychologist it was illegal for me to do so (see also FOF$_4$). Some say that it was just for the latter reason that **T.H.E.Y** did this and that the former reason I gave is just evidence of me overly dramatizing my stuff. To which I say, could be so … but … **FACT** remains: **I** *am* the *source* of my ideas, not the State—that is, *individuals* are the *source* of all good, not the State.

Of course, some non-existent god is not the source either.

That is, in what seems to be a never ending battle between Church and State for *control* of our pocketbooks, i.e. for control of *that* which controls our pocketbooks—*our minds*—the Church and State authorities down through the ages seem to take turns trying to convince us that T.H.E.Y are the soul-*source* of the *good* and we individuals are the sole-source of evil (puns intended). Thanks to Ayn Rand and Objectivism I predict that the Church & State's game—that is, T.H.E.I.R game—in America will be up or at least cross over the 50/50 bridge-of-no-return up around 2036 … or so. (See RaIseBooks and BiO Spiritualism NewsLetters Archive—doorsign.biz — December 2008 BiO Spiritualism NewsLetter Chart 5.)

(Calculations for the 2036 date in Chart 5 were made by me but I can't find them. I will try and find them and include them in some f.u.t.u.r.e writing—hopefully they were not lost in one of the two less than 100% recovered hard drive crashes I've had since I did them circa the mid 90's.)

Copies of correspondences between me and my lawyer about this *State-of-Minnesota-trying-but-failing-to-make-me-a-jailbird* **event** are available upon request (gary@raisebooks.com).

FOF₂
(circa 2006)

Minnesota Psych Board letter exchange of me *responding* to their call for input on new rules for psychologist licensing. As part of this exchange I opportunistically used it to get it on the record that I *legitimately* failed to pass the State of Minnesota's written exam for becoming a licensed psychologist that I *succumbed* to taking during an earlier time period (spring of 2001 post a family run business failure when family was getting dangerously poor and I was succumbing to family pressures to get a good paying job) and that I did **not**—either consciously or subconsciously—*purposely* fail the exam just so I could have something to rail against The State about. That is, FACT is I failed the exam fair and square so to speak (though to be fair to myself, I didn't study one second for it and also had I been in Texas I'd 'ah been damn close to passing). I didn't fail the exam just to create an artificial antagonist, a personal obstacle, something to push against.

Copies of correspondences between me and *The State of Minnesota Board of Psychology* about *this* **event** are available upon request (gary@raisebooks.com).

FOF₃
(circa 1993)
RaIse™ method's Blue Brochure
(see raisebooks.com)

How NOT to throw the baby out with the bathwater ...

... this brochure is a diagrammatic representation showing you how to NOT throw the baby out with the bathwater when you use *your* **capacity-to-reason** to *undo* those psychhological developmental errors that you made using that very same reasoning capacity. This Brochure will help you be a better psychhotherapist, that is, a better help-yu-help-yorself-therapist. FACT is psychhological problems require help to solve—be it self-help or other-help or both.

The Blue Brochure is available at raisebooks.com

FOF₄
(circa 1990)

MI Theory & Therapy Newsletters (also source for State's claim against me as highlighted in FOF₁) & Yellow Page ads for *STI Counseling Services*. FACT is my first Newletter did use the word psychological counseling services and I was only certified by The State to be—via a State certification form that I applied for and submitted and that "certified" me as—an Unlicensed Mental Health Provider.

Copies of these early articles and newsletters are available upon request (gary@raisebooks.com).

FOF$_n$
(circa future)

FOF$_{f.u.t.u.r.e}$

Appendix B

PS

Ayn Rand is wrong

on yet another point:

Selfishness is not *a* virtue.

Selfishness is a ___CARDINAL___ virtue.

Appendix C
PPS

Branden is wrong

(I believe I can *eventually* prove) on at least three points—three points that I am only going to list at this time as means to getting this started and not prove them at this time but plan to do so in the f.u.t.u.r.e (see Index, **Branden** for page numbers herein where I have more than once *praised* Dr. Branden for being the *good* psych(h)ologist that he is). The list below is intended to be my guardian list protecting me from the occupational **hazard** we humans faced known as *authoritarianism*—arguing with ourselves and/or others that something is true BECAUSE so 'n so says so.

Dr. Branden's three errors:

1. **his view of synergy** … (the whole is greater than the sum of the parts in the sense that you can't *predict* the whole just from a consideration of its parts. This view is no doubt a giant improvement over reason's enemies who erroneously advocate that synergy means/proves that *the whole is greater than the sum of its parts*, but it—Branden's improved definition—is still not the final correct view.)

2. **his view of life energy** … (too élan vital like)

3. **his complementary praise of Irvin D. Yalom, M.D.** page 94 *Honoring the Self*, hardcover, Jeremy P. Tarcher, Inc. Los Angeles, 1983 on the heels of criticizing Dr. Yalom, page 93. Since I had Dr. Yalom's book, "*Theory and Practice of Group Psychotherapy*" (Second Edition, Basic Books, Inc.,

Publishers, New York, 1975) as the textbook for one of my college classes in pusuit of my Masters Degree in Counseling Psychology I have some first hand experience with Dr. Yalom, qua Psychology Intellectual. My *psycho-hermeneutic* take (reference **Yes**, keyword: psycho-hermeneutics) on Dr. Yalom is this.

Metaphorically speaking Dr. Yalom is President and CEO of what could be labeled *College Kids Incorporated* who *use* group therapy as an ***opportunity*** to turn *individuals* into *collectivists* and/or as a *maintenance* strategy to help all collectivists maintain their "individual" souls in a *collectivistic* state. The pro-Yalom ' … is brilliant in so many ways … ' *complement* of Dr. Branden's stems, I suspect, from his Formal/*Professional* Secular Humanist bent (see **Yes**, page 92 for more) and it is really a bazar event as Dr. Branden is the one who identified—in spades!—the ***proper*** role of psychotherapeutic ***group*** therapy in the *individual's* development when he characterized it—"Psychology" Group Therapy—as *individual therapy in a group setting*. Dr. Yalom's work in this area, by contrast, could be labeled *Group Indoctrination in a Group Therapy setting*. And let me add this in-spades comment for your in-spades benefit just in-case you are in a **group** therapy that is ***not*** *individual therapy in a group setting*—if this then, *get out now!*

But, of course, if not then not. If it *is* **individual** therapy in a group setting then stay in it as long as you *are* getting personal, individual, *selfish* benefit from it—when this ends, move on.

(This entry #3 occasioned me to revisit my quarter of a century absence from Yalom's work. Of course there is *some* good in his material, but to refer to it as "brilliance" is a bit over generous since Yalom's biggest lack is that of integration. *Brilliance without integration* is a contradiction in terms.)

Now that I think about it maybe this number 3 should be: *Dr. Branden is wrong on his Formal/Professional Secular Humanist bent.*

Dunno, maybe … tbd (see f.u.t.u.r.e).

(If any Yalom driven group therapies produce a preponderance of individual group members who emerge from the group with a "hey, selfishness *is* a virtue" sentiment then I stand corrected in my psycho-hermeneutic take on Dr. Yalom.)

Appendix D
FPS

Moi is wrong

(maybe) about his view on *irrational* selfishness. That is, "He" (I) thought and wrote from his (my) day one (see *MI Theory and Therapy* FOF_4, Appendix A) that "rational selfishness" is redundant and "irrational selfishness" a contradiction in terms.

And so I will concede **the** (I-might-be-wrong) point to this fact: if a person accepts altruism—the belief that putting others before self *more-often-than not* is in one's self interest, so that, if this then—such a person could be said to be *irrationally* selfish.

But outside of this context *rational* and *irrational* selfishness are as I thought from day one—*redundant* and *a contradiction in terms*, respectively.

Glossary

A is A … one of the three axiomatic concepts of Ayn Rand's Philosophy of Objectivism; A is A means a thing can't be what it is (A) and what it isn't (non-A) at the same time and in the same respect. The attempt to **make** things be A and non-A at the same time and in the same respect is the attempt to **make** square circles. See Contradictions.

Altruism … is the philosophy that says when you have a choice you *should* choose to satisfy others' needs over your own needs more often than not with *more often then not* understood to mean 51% *or more* of the time whenever you have this choice—and with *or more* understood to mean, *better*.

Biocentric psychology … is the true science of psychology which defines psychology (see Branden, *The Psychology of Self Esteem*, Nash, 1969, p. 3) as … *the science that studies the attributes and characteristics which certain living organisms possess by virtue of being **conscious***. (italics, original emphasis; added emphasis, mine). Biocentric psychology and Contemporary psychology *are* competing views of what constitutes *true* psychology. It is my contention that ***Contemporary*** psychology is to ***Biocentric*** psychology what alchemy is to chemistry, what Ptolemy's astronomy was to Copernicus' astronomy, what false is to true.

Blue Brochure – a kind of "wiring schematic"—or rather, *re-wiring schematic* to be precise—showing how I used *my* growing *knowledge* of psycHology to stitch together—after the fashion of a cross-over pattern like that of the lacing on an American football—*my* re-developing *psychhoepistemological* self as I was determined—come hell or high water—to become an *autonomous*, *selfish*, *self-responsible*, *authentic* self-esteeming *individual*. A metaphorical football as it were as stand-in for my literal brain held in front of me in both hands at chest height with me looking down atop the stitching atop the ball as if I (by mental will) was back 'n forthing stitching together my new (psychhoepistemological) self. And as such, I was setting my life course to *produce* evermore happiness for me here on this planet while I actually lived and breathed. Just as, *ultimately*, only I can make me happy so too— *ultimately*—only you can make you happy. For the Blue Brochure link see $FOF_{n=3}$ Appendix A. (And NOTICE the statement above: *"only you can make you happy"* because it is a *truism* of such import that it *should* be considered a Principle. Consequently, on the way to making it be-so-in-*my*-mental-universe I plan to treat it as a "theorem" in f.u.t.u.r.e books and especially in those on *Theoretical PsycHHology*.)

Brain – *organ of integration* of external sensory data into **percepts** and (possibly also) of internal frequency data from all physiological inputs into a harmonious "musical" score (this last is more Theoretical PsycHHology speculation–e.g., brain is conductor; internal organs are violins, oboes, trumpets, cymbals and so on). Brain's other function is as *Consciousness'* mind/matter device: e.g., I *will* my little toe to wiggle and this little piggy … etc., all the way home. (The **Mystics** search for the "ability" to use mind-over-matter to *bypass* the *actual* matter-muscles of our bodies to bend spoons is an example of an M in the DIM View Model of developing man—see DIM below. The **BM Materialists'** search for an automatic organ of survival that they can control—i.e. the made brain—is an example of a D. I of course as evinced by all my writings—ISBN'd books and all web content —am an example of an "I"—pun intended.)

Certainty is a psycHological state. It is the psycHological state of knowing and it does not distinguish between true and false, it only distinguishes between *certain* and *not* certain. True or false is the providence of reason; certainty is the providence of you and your real psychology. You in this context is your *personal identity* and your personal identity is *you*. (For example, see brain discussion above and consider: in the literal case of a "made" man in the Mafia—reference Wikipedia description—could such a "man" kill and murder without being "certain" that he is right? *Objectively* he is wrong as reason demonstrates, but in his own mind he is *certain* he is right—if not he could not act. In similar "reasoning" fashion cognitive neuroscientists are "certain" that the brain and consciousness are one in the same or that the brain is the seat of consciousness and if neither the same nor seat then it's because consciousness does not exist—it is not a *something*. Voila! the brain is **made** to be what "they" burn the midnight oil to **make** it be 'rathern what it is—a physical organ—with identifiable physiological properties including my speculations about its vibratory prowess (if true) and any other to be discovered (true) physiological thingys—nothing more, nothing less.)

Contemporary psychology … see Psychology below and also in Nomenclature.

Consciousness is conscious … another one of the three axiomatic concepts of Ayn Rand's Philosophy of Objectivism. For more see <u>**Yes's**</u> Chapter 3 and Chapter 17 (p. 171) and/or Ayn Rand and the Professional Objectivists (aynrand.org). See also RaIse Books and BiO

Spiritualism archive article (doorsign.biz): *Breaking News: X-factor discovered*, August 30, 2012:

> Consciousness is a thing-like-thing that to be understood must be owned. And the price of ownership is: *respect.*

Consciousness to be owned must be respected.

That is, **now** we can *expand* on the *metaphor* (**Yes** p. 61, footnote #49) which is a *concretization* of the idea that mind and body are a unity: ... *body is the sponge saturated with the water of consciousness* ... by **adding**:

> *and* **I** *am the owner of it all.*

And we can and will go one step further here before we stop. We can MAKE a conscious (reverse) "slip" (as it were, reference **Yes** page 285) by turning our awake peripheral sense (as "we" wrote the above) of the word 'tower' surrounding the word 'owner' into a "slip" and conclude that perhaps in dreams, or at minimum in *my* dreams—and, notwithstanding a preexisting standing order of mine not to do this, maybe "we" can even postulate a dream universal—super duper tall buildings, i.e., tower like structures are the result of our subconscious perceptual mechanism (under the control of the art function) churning out visual aids (pictures) of abstractions ... that is:

... body is the sponge saturated with the water of

consciousness and **I** *am the* tow*n*er *of it all ...*

*(Damn ... this is fun ... don't you just love it? And I ask yu, is there any language equal to let alone better than English for us to use in growing and developing our **introspective** self?)*

Contradictions … do not exist. Nature *demonstrates* this to us by not having any.

DIM Hypothesis – D isintegration, I ntegration, M isintegration, as in Dr. Peikoff of *The Ominous Parallels/End of Freedom in America* fame takes a DIM view of the "occupational hazards" facing developing humans. (see amazon.com/author Leonard Peikoff for more). Integration, "all" agree—that is, *both* Professional Objectivism as represented here by Dr. Peikoff *and* True Scientific Psychology as represented by Dr. Branden elsewhere agree, ***integration***—*is the hallmark of human intelligence at any and **all** levels of human development.* And based on my own personal, **_first_** hand experience I couldn't agree more and want to add: "integration" doesn't *require* intelligence, it *produces* it.

Dipolar man … a ***hypothesis*** from (my) *Theoretical PsycHHology* that states that man**, *by nature*,** is emotionally di-polar and so, in the action realm—the place where unobstructed emotions terminate—man is best thought of as Two Dimensional Man. That is, 2D healthy man only moves in one of two *fundamental* directions **at-a-time** *all the time*, and by implication, unhealthy, discombobulated man tries to move in both directions **at-the-same time** *all the time* and usually ends up—as he or she must given that the impossible is impossible—either going nowhere or spinning around in circles out of control. The two *most* fundamental—can't be reduced further— directions of course are those identified by the Professional Objectivist Dr. Harry Binswanger (qua amateur scientist, professional thinker) when he argued (see his *Selected Topics in the Philosophy of Science* audio Tape 1, side B from Second Renaissance Books, Oceanside, California 1991) that the primary directions for man are: *not* up-

down, right-left but rather, " … *to* and *from* … ". To
which we now can add that the two most fundamental
actions for man: *towards* and *away* come from the two
most fundamental—can't be reduced further—*emotions*:
love and *fear*. (For examples of beings without fear always
moving *towards* see the canine species and for examples of
beings overwhelmed with fear and hence always moving
away see the feline one. For examples of beings with both
love and *fear* as well as all the—plus and minus, positive
and negative—*actionable* derivatives thereof, see the
human species.) Though the implications here for modern,
contemporary psychology's (**erroneous**) *view* of mentally
ill bi-polar man are obvious they are beyond our current
scope and so will not be dealt with here but will be dealt
with in a later work. To anticipate the "direction" of this
f.u.t.u.r.e work see *www.biospiritualism.com* and its
identification from 5/15/2005 that *emotions*—in the
mathematical or rather physical or rather teleömetric or
rather all-of-the above *science* sense—are *vectors*.

Egoism … from a Philosophy of PsycHology point of view
and hence *in the **science** of psycHHology, **egoism*** is the
belief that there is something inside of us that cannot—
metaphysically cannot—escape the reality of our choices.
And further, that that something *is* what I call, *ego*. See
self.

Emotions—from a psycHHometric, that is, teleömetrics
viewpoint—emotions are One-Directional vectors
produced by the consciousnesses of human beings.
(Animals can physically feel but not emote—humans can
and do do both. Also animals cannot *not* act against their
feelings. For proof, see your cat running upstairs to hide
under the bed every single Tuesday morning without
exception when the loud and noisy garbage truck comes

trundling down the road and/or at every clap of thunder each and every time—without fail. And then notice: *humans* can and do act against their emotes whenever they think they *should*—they can stand their ground and pause long enough to *identify*: 'oh sh.. that's a garbage truck, it's not dangerous' … or … 'that's thunder … an approaching storm … it could be dangerous … be alert.').

Engineering is the *application* of science to the problem of making man-made things work in reality—of ***making*** the statement, *it works **in theory** AND **in practice*** a **true** statement. (For humans of course this is a rather large "occupational hazard" so to speak and one for which the animals below man don't have to face. See **Yes's** criticism of contemporary—that is, wrong—psychology for more. See also *Three Theoreticals* below.)

Existence exists … is the first axiomatic concept of Ayn Rand's Philosophy of Objectivism. Existence exists means existence is eternal and ***everything*** is *inside* of existence, even time.

evil: All that which **destroys** that *which is proper to the life of a rational being* is the evil.

FOF**$_n$ = **Facts on File …(see Appendix A) … a collection of information demonstrating to my readers that I'm not making the particular (FOF$_n$ - tagged) stuff up (n is neither cardinal nor ordinal but just a nominal number. That is, n is being used as a unique identifier number/label/name to locate a particular FOF in the listing.)

Future is everybody's future, ***f.u.t.u.r.e*** is mine—my *specific* future ***as will be determined*** by me **now** and my **now** choices—including my course correction choices now

and in the future. (Inside the physical context of course of
me living on the 3rd rock from the sun along with other
humans and their f.u.t.u.r.e.s).

Galt's Speech for blank entries link and discussion herein
in Chapter 6. (See *Atlas Shrugged*, Part III, Chapter VII
"THIS IS JOHN GALT SPEAKING," p. 1017, HC,
Eighteenth Printing, Random House, New York, 1957, by
Ayn Rand.)

good: All that which is required for man's survival in the
character of *being* man and/or *becoming* man is the good,
all that which destroys it is the evil.

hgtikoi (see *Nomenclature* for more) is pronounced, **high-
coy**, and it names an internal side thought that is important
to *our* interests and is noticeable by us if our *self
awareness* ability is of a high order—that is, is high
"enough" to catch and then be extra-aWare of the
particular thought and recognize it for what it is: ***important
to us***.

The initials (h-g-t-i-k-o-i) come from a client experience of
mine from a young mother who said she heard it from one
of the three smartest people she knew during the time
frame when she was raising her kids.

> She and her husband were driving in the car
> with their two and three year old daughters
> and four year old son. They were taking the
> son to a day care program being held in
> their local park.

… as she told it …

We were driving west on a main thoroughfare approaching
the intersection of another main road with our destination
being to drop off our son at a one-hour summer day care
event located at the opposite end of the northwest diagonal
from the intersection we had to stop for the red light at.

It was a warm and cheery summer morning.

My husband was driving and stopped at the light and
asked—in his usual indecisive way—to the sky above and
to me (riding shotgun) if he should go right here to get to
the park or go straight ahead? I said I'm not sure it
matters. Our four year old son—strapped in his car seat
behind my husband—said, "go straight ahead" and my
husband seemed not to hear and kept muttering and
wondering which way to go. Then everybody except our
two year old daughter was telling my indecisive husband
what to do at the same time: I said, "It doesn't matter, go
right go straight ahead either is ok". My son reiterated that
we should go straight ahead and then our two year old
daughter apparently decided to speak because we heard
this little female voice from the car seat behind me say,
"*hey guys this is kind of important*". And we all stopped
with subdued chuckles under our breath. What is? I asked
and she said, "This is not the way to Duffy's".

We laughed and said what do you mean? and she said
"Duffy's is back that way", as she pointed to the back
window and we lightly laughed again. We aren't going to
Duffy's right now … is that where you want to go for
lunch today as we can surely go there later … and she said,
yes.

Long story short my client said, "Duffy's—a back to the
50's style restaurant that we hadn't been too with the kids
in over a month—*was* located in the direction that our

daughter was pointing to—which was direct opposite to the direction we were travelling."

And then after thinking about this she said I thought, wow that's pretty *smart* for a two year old to have such a good recollection of the correct direction to a favorite restaurant. For god's sake, she at 2 years old strapped into a car seat in the back seat of our car couldn't even see out the window, how did she know where that restaurant was located?

After my client had left and later on when I reflected on this event it dawned on me that the two year old in that story was totally into her own thing and she not interested one iota in which way they were traveling for her 4 year old brother's park 'n rec event located in their local Park— she wanted to go to Duffy's to eat (she liked their french fries) so as far as she was concerned they were going in the "wrong" direction and neither right or straight ahead was "correct".

Of course she didn't say, hey dad you are wrong but rather she said, "hey guys this is kind of important" …

Also I thought, wow! we are witnessing the workings of her (f.u.t.u.r.e) subconscious mind in real (31 months old) CONSCIOUS MIND time … you could almost sense the cogs turning when she uttered "hey guys this is kind of important" with the obvious "to me" left out as it not *yet* part of her thoughts to think about anything other than what *is* important to her.

Longer story shorter, voila! high-coy as in h-g-t-i-k-o-i as in "h ey g uys t his i s k ind o f i mportant" … to *my* needs at this **exact** *point* in time.

That is, the two year old daughter in the vignette can't not yet *not* be aware of what is *important to her* because she hasn't yet "learned" that what's important to her doesn't count when compared to what's important to other people. (I say this last part now with a face that looks as sarcastically sarcastic and sneery as I can make it.)

So in conclusion my take away—besides the high-coy flag factor—is this: if you have a chance to hang around 1, 2, 3, 4 , 5 year olds I highly recommend that you do it and while you are pay particular attention to how *naturally* smart they are. In the above vignette the parents were experiencing their daughters tomorrow's subconscious today and, yes they did go to Duffy's for lunch later on that day and the daughter did order her french fries. And,

hgtikoi{{{Here is something therapists know that I don't think *all* parents know: children in their formative years between the ages of birth and six'ish are not only the smartest people on the planet but also the most precious.}}}

I of course as a Grandparent with three grandkids that I (and Grandma) did spend a lot of time around when they were in their formative years (we baby sat them one day a week for nearly two years in addition to normal family gettogether time) know first hand the truth of this *high-coy* moment.

Human Nature* Start (0)** … at this beginning point in reflecting on our ***development we do not know and we don't need to know WHAT our *human nature* is, we only know and we only need to know, THAT it is. And further, *that* as an existent "inside of existence" it has an identity.

***Human Nature* Next (+1)** … and that we as beings with a volitional, rational, conceptual consciousness have to figure out WHAT—in **addition** to volitional, rational, conceptual—*that* identity is.

Integration ... mental integration ... *Growing* our mental whole into a bigger whole that *matches reality* to the same or better degree as our current, existing totality of mental contents and mental actions that do match reality. If we "grow" it to match reality less that is disintegration not integration. Integration requires *same* OR *more* matches with *more* the *best* integration and 100% matching reality the *ultimate* integration. (The degree of our matching is the degree of our happiness.)

ISBN'd means a completed, finished books-in-progress manuscript of mine that is good enough (as viewed by me) to be published and is published with a specific ISBN and/or eISBN as the means of elevating the work to a higher standard (of mine) compared to other things I have "published"—e.g. web content without ISBN's. This points to my hierarchy of *good-better-best* writings of mine which in reverse order are: ISBN'd (best), my website content including my NewsLetters, my kindle pubs without ISBN's or eISBN's and my blog responses to others' blogs and blog-like writings, and on down to my everyday journal entries--the good, my good starts (in my mind of course, but it starts) its first appearance in reality as writings in my daily writing journals.

Isn't Everyone Selfish?—the article by Nathaniel Branden in the Ayn Rand book "The Virtue of Selfishness" at amazon.com by the same title. In the article Dr. Branden demonstrates that the philosophically correct answer to the question is: No, they are not and consequently, no one is deserving of such a *compliment* without *earning* it.

jot's – self functions judging, observing, testing

kjv = gKGV = *The King James Version of The Christian Holy Bible as remembered AND interpreted by me.* Though technically I am not *vehemently* against Christianity as **interpreted** by others, I am **passionately** against it as interpreted and applied by me as I was born into it and raised in it as a Lutheran. Specifically, I was raised as a Missouri Synod Lutheran. Missouri Synod Lutherans have *The King James version of The Holy Bible* as their "bible". Since I was a conscientious human being from the day I was born—I *surmise* based on *one* memory recall of a serious me trying to learn/memorize a few words from a strip of white paper like that of a Chinese fortune cookie to say in a Christmas program at our Church when I was 3 years old and on some "geometric" dreams I recall having at an age less than 3... I think ... therefore that I was very conscientious from a very very early age and so—I read that bible from cover to cover *twice* by the time I was 9 years old. When I tell this to people today they say, 9? really? and then I say well, figuratively speaking perhaps. As I could maybe have started at 9'ish and finished around 12'ish as that is the age wherein I completed phase 2 of the christian indoctrination. Phase 2 for me was two years of catechism at the end of which when I was 12 or 13 years old I was officially—with pomp and circumstance—*confirmed into-the-faith* by the authoritarian powers that be (the presiding Minister, deacons and other church helpers and other adults sitting in the pews observing and morally sanctioning the beginning of my spiritual demise ... **but** what's that phrase? ... oh, I know: Thank god for Ayn Rand!). Since that time of course I not only have done a major *rejection* of the Christian *faith* but I have also *purged* same from my very own soul. This last is *not* figurative but rather *is* literal. See SVTOUL for more and don't kid your(christian-if-same-applies-to-you)self:

happiness without purging is severely limited but with a proper purge happiness is unlimited or at least is not of necessity *significantly* more limiting than that which may or may not be set by our natural human natures. (Proper purging, per my experience, makes it ***possible*** for all Social Metaphysicians to become Metaphysical Metaphysicians or in the parlance of Ayn Rand for all second handers to *become* first handers.)

Knowing is the providence of philosophy. And, *notwithstanding* thousands upon thousands and perhaps even millions of graves of dead philosophers (of a certain ilk be they amateur or professional), we humans *can* and *do* know things. And we know things with certainty because a non-certain knowing is a contradiction in terms. See contradictions.

Mental health … is the unobstructed capacity for reality-bound cognitive functioning—and the exercise of this capacity.

Mental illness … is the sustained *impairment* of this [mental health] capacity.

myCountryRoadExercise: a Biocentric Psychotherapy exercise led by Dr. Nathaniel Branden in one of his weekend intensives in the late '70's that I was a participant in (the words are not verbatim, they are just my general recollection of them):

Breathe and relax.

And breathe and relax some more.

Then tighten the muscles in your legs and clenched fists and upper arms and body and hold … 1 … 2 … 3 …

and release instantly and then repeat: tense-hold-release
…. then again and … again … and so on …

What I remember is doing this until you are in a
meditative relaxed state … then while maintaining this
state imagine yourself out in the country leisurely
walking down a country road.

As you walk along you see the trees and green grass,
smell the country's fresh air as it blows ever so softly
through the trees on its way to somewhere down the
road.

You notice what looks like a person standing by one of
the larger trees located by the side of the road quite a
ways ahead of you.

You continue walking at the same leisurely pace,
knowing that eventually you will make it to the tree and
that person and then you will be able to identify who it
is.

You stroll along and wonder with increasing excitement
and mystery: who is that standing there leaning up
against that big oak tree?

You get closer … you see what appears now to be a
very young boy [or girl to match whichever is your sex]
and you walk closer.

Finally you get to the tree and say hi to the little boy
and ask him some …

Halt.

Pause.

For me—and to explain my context—in this intensive
exercise I have to mention that I was primed for this
particular excise because prior to coming to this
intensive (a 2000 mile flight, 4 day weekend trip for me

from my Minnesota residence to Branden's California Hotel conference room where he hosted this particularly intense weekend intensive) I had done some introspective work on my own via analyzing dream content and other self-help practices. As I was want to do to continue my looking into all the potential benefits from being ever more educated in Biocentric Psychology's 3 R's—that is, the 4 SA's—that is, *self-awareness, self-acceptance, self-assertion and self responsibility.*

From my dream journal I recalled the time I had discovered an inner attitude of mine that amounted to me discovering an inner cry-baby baby who felt sorry for his(read my)self—which was something I did do to my detriment. And deciding at the time upon awakening and thinking about it that what I wanted to do, what I ***needed*** to do was "get at that little bastard and kill him off once and for all" as metaphor/means for finishing off my bullshit attitude about self pity. Well that really didn't produce much productive psych(h)ological benefit for me at the time so when months later in this country road exercise I was able to sense and "see" the little me, the young me standing by that tree.

Had I not been "primed" I'm not sure—given my "macho" attitude—that I would have accepted Dr. Branden's suggestion to go with the exercise.

But I did ... and long story short: me and the little guy became good buds and I swooped him up in my arms and flew him and me back to the present where Dr. Branden brought us slowly back into the room and asked people to comment on the experience.

There was a lot of excitement in the participants who got into the exercise and it included me but I did not share as such was not my nature to do back then.

Now of course some say I share too much.

Perhaps, but ….

I'm sure you get my drift.

Good luck on this if you decide to try it on your own or have your own therapist pilot you there for your own self discoveries.

Ego re-integration is what this felt like to me at the time (which was I believe the 'theme' of the exercise). Following this intensive I felt stronger, my weak ego was less so, that is, it was not only *less* weak but it was **also** *more* strong. (I had lifted weights when in college for my own physical strengthening and this felt just like that except it had to do with my *ego* not my muscles.)

If you were/are like I was and want more ego building exercises try Branden's Basic Relaxation and Ego Strengthening procedures tape as I found this at the time to be very very helpful also—that is, back in the '70's, that is, back in my thirtysomethings.

Pscyh(h)otherapy works—that is, the *correct* kind does. I have no comments here about the incorrect kinds. (Other than, see Appendix C for more.)

Objectivism … *The Philosophy of Ayn Rand,* see aynrand.org for more.

payne = psycHological pain, search same as keyword in my first ISBN'd book: *Yes. (Is BiO Spiritualism the answer?)* See **Yes** below.

Personal identity comes **before** your *personality* and whereas your personality is the means by which others know you, your *personal identity* is the means by which you know you.

Personality, qua that part of your personal identity that you *allow* others to see, along with all your *physical* characteristics that others can see with or without your help is the means by which *others* know you.

Psychology, that is, one lowercase '**h**' erroneous psychology, that is *contemporary psychology* is three fundamental things: (1) the equation *brain is mind is brain* (2) the *science of behavior ... control ... of others* and (3) wrong. (Fundamental #2 is also—see Dipolar Man—a *hypothesis* from *Theoretical PsycHHology*: H_0: last century's (American) contemporary **psychology** was defined as: *the science of behavior*; this century's added the second part: "... *control of others*". Today's Contemporary Psychology is dedicated to **making** psychology **be** the <u>*science*</u> *of controlling the behavior of others*. For a fuller expose of these shenanigans see **Yes** below as well as doorsign.biz archive of BiO Spiritualism NewsLetters, especially the March 2012 one.)

*Psyc**H**ology*, that is, one capital '**H**' *true* science psycHology, that is the *Biocentric Psychology* of Dr. Nathaniel Branden, author of *The Psychology of Self Esteem* who is—per my assertion—the father-founder of the **true** *Science of Psychology*. Biocentric Psychology defines true psychology as the *science that studies the attributes and characteristics that certain living organisms possess by virtue of being conscious.* This *is* the true science of "psychology". See one lower case '**h**' contemporary "psychology" for an example of a false version.

PsycHHology is **H** uman PsycHology, hence it is the *science that studies the attributes and characteristics that human beings possess by virtue of their distinctive form of consciousness.* PsycHHology is the human component by itself separated out of your (total) PsycHology. Your real psychology (psycHology) entails all characteristics and aspects—animal and human—of your immutable human nature ("we" assume aspects below these—insect, amoebic, vegetative and on down are NOT purely psycHological but rather trail off by degrees into pure physiological). Your human nature is embodied in the seedling-you. As you grow and develop from that seedling into a born human and then an adult human your human nature is ever present and your (post-birth) *responses* to it forms the **foundation** of your *personal identity* and your continuing responses *ultimately* form your fully formed personal identity. (The adult you along with others can use your adult *personality* to help you gain insights into your actual personal identity. Such insights are good because ultimately no one—with one exception—can understand you to the degree you *need* to be understood. The exception is: you, *you* are the *only one* who can understand you to the degree, to the depth you *need* in order to enjoy *your* life to its fullest.)

PsycHHology Engineering is *applying* the Science-of-Self-In-The-Universe—that is, applying *Theoretical PsycHHology*—to the problem of making self's psycHology work in reality. If it doesn't work then your choice is to change your real psychology or change reality. Since reality is immutable and real reality redundant, if changing it is always your first choice then that by itself is *proof* that it is your psycHHology that needs to be changed. (Since one's psychhology is in large part one's applied philosophy this (pen)ultimately means: *change your philosophy*. And since philosophy means, metaphysics, epistemology and ethics this *ultimately* means: **change for the better not worse**—that is, **make better**, that is, **make match reality** better—your metaphysic, your epistemology and your ethic. That is, I had to and so do you.)

Self ... is *either* ego's friend *or* ego's enemy; which, is up to you. See *ego* under egoism.

Selfishness ... *is a virtue.*

s.k.y ... another example of the dot technique as same is idiosyncratically used by me to honor the self by honoring *one* of self's many capacities (in this particular case, my *creative* capacity) ... also as a point of psychoepistemology in action we can jump to the first page of Chapter 11 and see my technique of turning **sky** into **s.k.y** by way of a previously made conscious suggestion (of mine) to (my) subconscious that maybe, just maybe "cliché's" are clichés for a reason and as such they might, just might contain deeper meaning. *'So subconscious—if yu don't mind—take the time (once in awhile) to look for deeper meaning in clichés—especially since it appears as if I sure like to use them, so look for deeper meaning— and/or CREATE it.'* So, what does **s.k.y** stand for? I don't know ... let's see ... hum, ah, ... hum .... s elfishness k isses y ou ????? Hey, what the hey, why not: Selfishness Kisses Yu. I love it. Sounds great. Good job.

STI ... *Selfishness Training Institute*, see Appendix A.

Social Metaphysicians & Metaphysical Metaphysicians
… see teleömeter inside **psycho-epistemology** inside
Gary's Venns inside **gdeering.com**.

SVTOUL …*Spiral Vortex Theory of UnLearning*, another
to be developed theory within Theoretical PsycHHology.
The SVTOUL theory is the answer to the psychhological
question: *How DO you purge the irrational from your
very own soul?* For more see **f.u.t.u.r.e** (not here in
Glossary, but the real one subsequent to the publication
date of this ISBN'd book = 978-0-9774996-1-8 = this book
here = the one you are holding in your hand and/or field of
view).

Teleömetrics … is the *name* of the to be developed science
of measurement for the science of psycHHology. Naming
something is usually the last step not the first but since
contemporary one h psychology is so f'd up and has as its
measurement science the science named *psychometrics*
"we" have to make it abundantly clear that our
psychhological measurement—or even psycHological
measurement—does ***not*** mean *psychometrics* and
psychometrics does not mean the measurement of human
psychhological units—whatever those are because we
haven't yet determined *what* they are. That is, we haven't
yet so determined beyond what Ayn Rand has hinted at in
her description of teleometric measurement – graded
relationship of means to ends, etc. — and what she has
referred to as the *proper* attributes for *measuring*
consciousness – see Ayn Rand for more, especially
Objectivist Epistemology book(s)
(amazon.com/AynRand/Introduction to Objectivist
Epistemology). For now my working definition is:

teleömetrics, qua the mathematics of introspection, is the science of the psychhological measurement of-the-self *by-the-self.*

TFA – ego *functions* thinking, feeling, acting as *capacities* and in the character of *self actualizations* are *particular* thoughts, *particular* feelings, *particular* acts …

TFAjot's – yin and yang of ego-self-ego-self-ego-self leap-frogging through conditional life. (See *TFA.* See *jot's*)

Three Theoreticals & one Integration, see following:

> *Theoretical God … says …* I **need** a mechanism to protect man from himself when he errors … voila! I will name it "guilt".

> *Theoretical Philosophy … says …* guilt **SHOULD** *subdue* self assertiveness …

> *Theoretical PsycHHology* …after *observing* real living people … concludes … guilt DOES subdue self assertiveness …

> *Theoretical Integration*/**Psychhological Principle:** Guilt subdues self assertion *as it should.* Guilt is the resultant emotion that comes from violating in action one of my own standards of behavior regardless of the objectivity of that standard so I better goddamn well **make** my standards be objective—that is, **match reality**—least I spend all my time on this earth feeling guilty over internalized non-objective (mis-matched to reality) standards.

TLC – **Tender Loving Care,** means considerate and solicitous care; caring for something so much that you take all the time required to nurture it and protect it so that it turns out to be the best that *you* can make it be. Covers everything *from* raIsing children to be on track for becoming the world's best—i.e., most selfish—adult human beings on-down the scale *to* one of your offspring say becoming a baker and raising bread dough for the purpose of making the world's best bread.

Vectors: physical quantities that have *both* a scalar magnitude and a directional component, e.g. some rocket engine exhaust as 12 thousand pounds of thrust directed *downwards* versus physical quantities that have only a *scalar* quantity, e.g. a *dozen* rockets.

Yes refers to my **first** ISBN'd book: *Yes. (Is BiO Spiritualism the answer?)* ISBN 978-0-9774996-0-1, available on Amazon.com and RaiseBooks.com in the aBook version (soft cover both places) and the eBook version for the Kindle on Amazon.com.

yu: *ego's separation* way (without detachment—see the literal Blue Brochure) of referring to the *self* half of us and vice versa, the *self's* separation way (also without detachment) of referring to the *ego* half of us … *yu* is in contradistinction to the personal pronoun "*you*" which refers to other selfs in the world at-large external to the *integrated* me, myself and I *ego-self-me*.

(As a person who is highly practiced in the *Art of Introspection* I can *sense* who is calling who *yu* in any such usage—be it written or inner dialogue thoughts. You cannot think me to have a monopoly on this "sense" anymore than you would think me to have a monopoly on a "sense" of humor. Human beings—with the human form of consciousness that we do have—have these "senses" and like many if not all of our *attributes* of consciousness they are extendible, learnable, trainable … enhanceable … expandable … improvable … growable.

Useable.

That is, if there was a god, which there isn't, but if there was I sure would like to say to him or her or it: thanks a bunch for all our *wonderful* human attributes—humans are just the greatest, aren't they? (**Yes.**)

PsycHHology books by Gary Deering

RELEASED

Yes. (Is BiO Spiritualism the answer?) ISBN 978-0-9774996-0-1, LCCN 2005910403, RaIse Books Publisher, October 6, 2006.

<u>RELEASED</u>

<u>Selfish'ism (Get up off your deathbed and save yourself brother. I had to and so do you.)</u> ISBN 978-0-9774996-1-8; RaIse Books Publisher, February 7, 2013.

f.u.t.u.r.e

PsycHHology Engineering's Selfish'ism vs. Social Engineering's Altruism, ISBN tbd; Release tbd; Working Title: *Selfish'ism II* ...

---

f.u.t.u.r.e

DiPolar Man AND Theoretical PsycHHology OR Vice Versa, ISBN: tbd, Release: tbd; Working Title: *BiO Spiritualism + Sasz vs. The Emperor (Contemporary) Psychology that has no clothes* ...

---

f.u.t.u.r.e

egoAerodynamics, ISBN: tbd, Release: tbd; Working Title: *Including the Kitchen Sink* ...

Gary Deering's websites and websides:

www.gdeering.com especially the webside, *Gary's Venns* which is my seminal website from the 20th Century (August 30th, 1998, to be exact).

www.aLogicalChoice.com for one out of an infinity of **R** choices in **WASHeRs** (**W** ork **A** rt **S** ex **H** uman relationships **e** xercise of our human capacities **R** ecreation as in Re-Creation and **s** ome oiatbd as in some other (pleasure sources in life) if any tbd).

www.BiOspiritualism.com **click through** and read the content and then at the bottom pause to let things sink in and then loop back to *simulate* going to bed at night and dreaming (or not, but for sure sleeping-resting-recharging) and then **waking up** the next morning in the same universe, same solar system, same planet, same continent-country-state-city-abode, albeit, a different "place" … a new day … to be … and to continue the life process … of living … and *being* … and *growing* … and *developing* … and … enjoying.

www.degageblog.com Gary's Blog

www.therealinconvenienttruth.com the US's quaternary Presidential Election of 2000 as demonstration of why cry babies can never see the truth. Because they are always too busy crying about the wrong things (crying about the right things is good, about the wrong things is bad). This website is arguing that a real incumbent party's Presidential Candidate would have said 'I *should* have beaten my opponent by a country mile but since I didn't, I

deserved to loose and I will re-evaluate myself and correct
my errors so that next time around I will do better and
win.' I do not know Mr. Gore personally but I do not think
this is what he said or if he did then he has a different
definition of what it means to win then do I. Mr. Gore, as
anyone can observe, is striving to become the high priest of
the Church of Environmentalism (link doorsign.biz June
2007 Newsletter/Global Warming) and from what I see in
the culture at large he seems to be doing pretty well in this
regard. But thank god he never got to be President, that is,
we for sure didn't need a budding druid in the white house
when 911 occurred.

www.BScounseling.com way to beat my (BiO
Spiritualism) critics to the punch, and since I have this
registry and pay for it I might as well use it and this is what
I did/do: use it to direct people to join our email list for
free BiO Spiritualism et al. NewsLetters and other
information …

www.doorsign.biz *Seek and ye shall find, knock and the
doors(ign.biz) shall be opened unto* you—the archive of
RaIse Books & BiO Spiritualism NewsLetters from 2007
forward. (This website *name* is an example of one thing
my ole'man always said about me when I was a kit … kid
… when I was a kid he always said, *'you can give that kid
a hammer and a nail and he'ul keep busy all day long'* …
it was said with a sense of endearment and though I
suspect it is some cliché from his generation, as a kid I
liked the praise as one who can make a lot out of a little
and have fun in the process. In line with this, the above
website name is one I had had for a different commercial
purpose and when that purpose failed I tried to sell the
name and when I couldn't sell it I thought of a use for it—a

thought that on my own terms I experienced as a flash of creativity—and so … voila! follow the link to see the use.)

www.cychhology.com .. direct link to Guest entry point into *Gary's Venns*.

www.GaryDeering.com direct link to **_Yes_** book on amazon.com

www.psychhology.com direct link to **_Yes_** *page* by itself dealing with my (first officially published) view of two 'hh' "psycHHology" as a concept; plus has a metaphorical definition of what *consciousness* (qua thing 2) is.

uu-uu-uu.oiatbd.com *f.u.t.u.r.e websites* (double u … etc. as one way to write a link in my word processor that will be a link some day but is not a link today, Monday, April 23, 2012 *specifically* but is for any general/specific day in the future); shorthand version is: *uuu.oiatbd.com*

Index

A

autonomous, 14, 42, 46, 102
Ayn Rand, *xii, xv, xix, 3, 25, 51, 63, 69, 72, 87, 95, 101, 103, 107, 108, 112, 113, 117, 121*

B

Biocentric Psychology, 52, 118
Branden,Nathaniel, xii, xviii, 23, 40, 52, 73, 80, 96, 97, 98, 101, 105, 112, 118

C

cardinal values, 8, 18, 46
consciousness, xv, 13, 15, 24, 27, 41, 51, 60, 77, 81, 104, 112, 119, 121, 123, 130
courage, 7, 31

D

development, 13, 14, 15, 17, 27, 33, 34, 35, 36, 37, 38, 39, 78, 87, 97, 105, 111
Dreams, xv

E

ego, *3*, 4, 7, 13, 18, 39, 63, 65, 66, 71, 72, 74, 78, 81, 106, 120, 122, 123
Egocentric, 13, 14
egoism, xxi, xxii, 106, 120
engineering, 44
Engineering, 107, 133
evil, 4, 5, 12, 25, 29, 37, 38, 39, 70, 85, 86, 87, 88, 89, 91, 107, 108

F

faith, 3, 24, 40, 41, 54, 113

G

goal, xxii, 22, 29, 30, 35, 40, 44, 61, 76
good, 9, xvi, xxii, 5, 10, 12, 19, 25, 26, 29, 37, 38, 39, 40, 42, 52, 62, 71, 73, 78, 83, 84, 85, 86, 87, 88, 89, 90, 91, 92, 96, 98, 108, 112, 119, 128

H

happiness, xxii, 11, 15, 18, 55, 61, 64, 68, 69, 72, 75, 81, 82, 83, 89, 102, 112, 114

I

individuation, 14
integration, xv, 14, 37, 98, 102, 105, 112
introspection, 4, 18, 28

J

joy, 11

M

moral, xxi, xxii, 12, 30, 31, 40, 71, 73, 83, 87

N

needs, xxii, 7, 9, 10, 11, 15, 18, 23, 24, 29, 30, 36, 63, 101, 119

About the Author

Honoring the self:
it's all about me, the author:
(see justification in the **PS** at the end here for using this hard to read script)

With the (self) publication of this (my second ISBN'd) book—*Selfishism*—I feel I can state unequivocally that I am a Biocentric Objectivist *to the core*. With the (self) publication of my first book: *Yes. (Is BiO Spiritualism the Answer?)* I invented *Biocentric Objectivism* and labeled it: *BiO Spiritualism*—the *process* of using philosophy (Objectivism) *and* psychology (Biocentric) to *make* **oneself** happy.

If the above seems spurious consider these facts.

Fact One: Today's Professional Objectivists to the man and to the woman denounce Dr. Nathaniel Branden, founder of *Biocentric Psychology*—the only *true* Science of Psychology that exists today.

Fact Two: Dr. Branden—psychologically speaking— left Objectivism in the dust many moons ago.

Fact Three: *Yes. (Is BiO Spiritualism the answer?)* exists. (And since today as I write this is November 29th, 2012 it has existed for more than six years.)

I have a Masters Degree in *Counseling Psychology* from the College of St. Thomas, St. Paul, Minnesota, USA (now the University of St. Thomas), and I also have a Bachelor's degree in *Aeronautical Engineering* from MIT (**M**innesota **I**nstitute of **T**echnology), University of Minnesota, Minneapolis, MN, USA.

St. Thomas was/is a traditional/mainstream school hence it taught more mainstream psychological thought. It did "allow" a lot of latitude in the kinds of writing that was required there for the *Masters Degree*. All my writing had an *Objectivist-Biocentric* viewpoint and I was *NOT* penalized for it. In fact, sometimes complimented. For example, one professor said (more than once...twice in fact) that he really looked forward to my papers: they were so interesting, no one had such a interesting slant on things, he said.

(Even though I took some refresher courses at the University of Minnesota I did not seek it out to get my advanced degree in Psychology because it was so solidly *Behaviorism* in its approach that I simply couldn't stand it. St. Thomas, in spite of its religious flaws, afforded me a kind of sanctuary as it were and I am/was/am still thankful for that and them.)

In my thirtysomethings I spent a couple hundred hours in the Self-Esteem intensives of Dr. Nathaniel Branden as well as many hours with other psychological therapies and therapists. I gained some selfish benefits (specifically in the area of emotional release and de-repression work) by working with several Scream/hug therapists, a bio-energetic neo-Reichian therapist and two co-facilitator marriage counselors who called themselves "eclectic" facilitators. I also spent time myself as an assistant "facilitator" of couples in marriage counseling and of individuals in both regular weekly Group sessions and in walk-in day centers for individuals in need of Crisis counseling *NOW* sessions.

But before this --that is, in 1968 and 1969-- I worked in my first professional career as an Aeronautical Test Engineer.

Here, qua part of the *unofficial* team that preceded President Reagan's Star Wars "program" I tested NASA and military satellites and their component parts for the *General Electric Company* qua a subcontractor to America's *official* Apollo Space Program. (Though I am "of" the Apollo and Woodstock era, I am not and was not a fan of the "hippie"/Woodstock mentality of that late '60's era. That is, of the idea that love is a cause and not an effect. I was and am a fan of "Apollo and Dionysus", the Ayn Rand article she wrote in that same time period about Apollo and Woodstock that argues that *ambition* --as exemplified by the Apollo Project-- is better than the *sloth* exemplified by Woodstock.)

(However, link here -
 http://www.gdeering.com/GarysVenns/ho5.htm - for what **also** was going on in the '60's via the "Woodstock" mentality that was beneficial for the older male children of that era in America—that is, in America qua superpower nation—that is, qua—by default—the policeman of the world—that is, it's a dirty job but somebody has to do it and if not a superpower then who?).

After the historic moon landing in 1969, I got out of the space business and spent the next 20 years instead as a computer hardware designer developing liquid-cooled protocols for supercomputers before I became a psychotherapist in private practice in the early 1990's.

After a couple of years as a psychotherapist and "licensed" *un-licensed* mental health provider I had a run in with the State of Minnesota over an issue of licensing. I wanted to stay un-licensed and call myself a psychologist and t.h.e.y. said "no way hoe-zay" and threatened to send me to jail, I said, screw that and-- left the business and became the money-man and computer-consultant and (6 hours one-on-one tutor trained) accountant-consultant behind my *second* wife as we started a General Contractor/Residential home building business which did really really well at first and which *almost* (as in god-damn near) made me my first million but which *in fact* ended in bankruptcy 10 years later. (And I reject the internalized charge that says since I virtually memorized every single sentence in Ayn Rand's novel "Atlas Shrugged" that I was really using it as a life-script and since I loved Reardon the best I was trying to be like him when he went bankrupt just before being truly free in a non-100%-laissez-faire-capitalistic world. ... like I said, I reject this claim for one simple reason: it ain't true. I went bankrupt for many reasons --three to be exact-- but this wasn't one of them. [link here for the three: http://www.gdeering.com/GarysVenns/AboutGary_FNy.htm])

So much for my money manness: making lots of money (that is, becoming rich) turned out to be much more difficult than I had (originally) thought.

Anyway, now I am back in the one-on-one personal growth self-help-via-the-written-word business and looking forward to writing more and more books for you to use as you attempt to achieve and perhaps even exceed the degree of happiness I have achieved *so far* in my life ... here on this planet earth ... *where* we actually live and breathe and exist.

PS

I use the above "curly-q" font type to *honor* the 12 year old in me who at some point in the 1957-58 school year in Triumph Minnesota, USA created that "curly-q" typeface for a 7th Grade Shop Class of his that had as an assignment to design something unique. Unfortunately I can't remember if it was literally to design a unique type face or if it was some other creative design project that I turned in with a cover page for it wherein I used this type face to title and explain my project.

Long story short I was reprimanded and made fun of by the Shop Class Teacher for using such a "goofy" style.

I of course was unable to defend myself and was a bit crushed by the *enthusiasm* with which I was denounced – and in front of the class.

To this day I don't know why the Shop Instructor acted this way towards me. At that time when I was 12—now that I think back about it—I don't think I was all that crushed—I just thought my instructor was a dork.

(Though the reason I'm not feeling that event now is because I did hear later on in my life that at some number of years after my trip through his classroom that he suffered some kind of mental breakdown and was carted off to the "nut" house. Whether this is literally true or not I don't know but *what I do know for sure* is I felt then— and I still do—that *if it was true* then it is some kind of poetic justice – or now, I guess, it's what some would call, Karma. And if it isn't true then I wonder: who the hell was it who told me this and why did I so easily accept it? Wait. For answer see sentence previous to question.)

But. What I don't like now is the thought that had I *followed through* I could have invented this font rather than the people who did "invent" it circa the 1990's (see Wikipedia, keyword, Curlz) some 30 years *after* I did!?!?!

But, truth be known I'm not 100% sure that I didn't get the idea from some of the 12 or 13 year old girls in my other classes of the time period who used this "style" to write their and their heartthrob's names on their spiral notebook covers.

(Or for that matter, in-the-loosest-possible-sense-possible see *Jungian Analytic Psychology* for insight

potential via his anima/animus "concepts" as the potential
source for my curly-q "creation".)

(Or not as the case may be.)

But, speaking of (green) spiral noteb … no … done …
don't go there … stop

The end.